New Brunswick Ghosts!Demons!

... and things that go bump in the Night!

by Dorothy Dearborn

illustrated by Carol Taylor

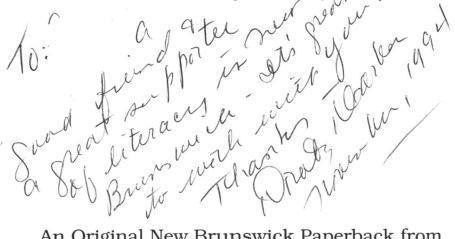

An Original New Brunswick Paperback from
Neptune Publishing Company Ltd., Saint John

A paperback original from Neptune Publishing Company Ltd.

First printing: September, 1994

The publisher wishes to acknowledge and thank the Department of Municipalities, Culture and Housing for their assistance in this publication.

Canadian Cataloguing in Publication Data

Dearborn, Dorothy 1927-
New Brunswick Ghosts-Demons ... and Things that Go Bump in the Night

ISBN 0-9692218-9-4
1. Ghosts -- New Brunswick. 1. Title
GR113. 5. N4D42 1994   398.25' 09715' 1 C94-950221-9

Cover Design by Carol Taylor and Dorothy Dearborn
Illustrations by Carol Taylor

Typesetting by Dearborn Group, Hampton, N.B.
Printed by The Tribune Press Ltd., Sackville, N.B.

Neptune Publishing Company Ltd.
116 Prince William Street, Box 6941
Saint John, NB. E2L 4S4

Acknowledgements

The people who have supported me in the research for this book are among the most interesting I have ever met. Each and every one possesses an alert and enquiring mind, open to adventure and information on every plane of existence. As a result, many have been able to lay claim to experiences as rare and exciting as those of any space traveller. Indeed, if Bob Wishart's perceptions are any indicator, the people they have met are far more than mere travellers in space, they are travellers in time.

Others, whose names do not appear for various personal reasons, have also made major contributions to this book. I wish to acknowledge at this time the very real contribution they have made. You know who you are. Thank you.

A very special thank you to Ned Belliveau, of Shediac and Moncton, who so generously gave me *carte blanche* to use material from his books and introduced me to the fascinating world of the Shediac of an earlier day.

The good graces of the CBC Radio Afternoon Shows in Saint John, Fredericton and Moncton are also appreciated. A particular thanks to Gary Middlehost and Harvey McLeod of CBC Saint John.

Thanks too, to Joanne Cadogan of the *Miramichi Leader.* Her story on my "Ghost Hunt" brought in a phenomenal response from an area rich in stories and people who are willing to share them.

It is impossible to name everyone who has encouraged and helped me with this work along the way, there have been too many to name all of them here, but the support of family and friends is greatly appreciated ... always.

Dorothy Dearborn
Hampton, NB
August 15, 1994

Other books by Dorothy Dearborn

Young Adult
The Secret of Pettingill Farms Avalon Books, New York
1972
The Mystery of Wood Island Avalon Books, New York
1973

Biographies
Give Me Fifteen Minutes Roy Alward of Havelock
Unipress Limited, Fredericton 1978
Dyslexia Dr. Arthur Chesley, Saint John
Dearborn Group, 1992

Anthologies
Willie
Stubborn, Strength, A New Brunswick Anthology
by Michael O. Nowlan, Academic Press Canada, 1983

Collections
Partners in Progress, New Brunswick
Atlantic Canada– At the Dawn of a New Nation
Windsor Publications Ltd. Burlington, Ontario, 1990

Non-Fiction
Unsolved New Brunswick Murders
Neptune Publishing Company Ltd. 1993

Contents

It's all in the family

When I first began researching the stories for this book I already had a store of material, stories that have been a part of my family through generations. I suspect we are all a bit fey because of our Scottish ancestry.

Exactly what we believe in is difficult to say. What we know is that life has another dimension beyond the here and now. What we don't know is Who? What? Why? Where? When? or How?

Does everyone have the potential to see into or experience that dimension?

I suspect so. Only time, and perhaps science, will tell us someday.

Forerunners and Extra Sensory Perception (ESP) , along with the occasional glimpse of a spirit "passing through" as it were, seem to be the norm with our family. Occasionally my mother (the late Huia Ryder) referred to these other world beings as her 'Ravens' the Biblical kind (I Kings 17: 4,5,6).

These guardian spirits did such things as tumble a stack of books to the floor in some dusty attic, ensuring the most rare and valuable appeared at her feet or to her hand. She also had a forerunner, a spirit who came to her during the night with news of an impending death.

Of course in our family there is always the humorous side to every story. Mother took for granted her ability to communicate through telepathy so never thought to question the validity of any communication that might arrive 'out of thin air', as it were. One day when involved in a chore our domestically challenged family avoids whenever possible ... scrubbing the kitchen floor ... she was not surprised to hear a neighbour's voice interrupting a music program to inform her of the death of a mutual friend.

"I just wanted to tell you that Mable died today," the voice said.

"Oh," said my mother. "I'm sorry to hear that. When is the funeral?"

The disembodied voice informed her of the pertinent details and mother thanked her and the music came back on.

That evening she was telling my father of her experience. He was of a more practical bent. He apologized for disillusioning her but explained what must have happened.

The out-of-time experience occurred in the days when radio was very new and exciting, crystal sets were the magic of the era. My father, who had an inventive mind, had rigged the earphones of a set into a glass tumbler placed on the kitchen table. The tumbler acted as a loud speaker so mother could be entertained as she scrubbed.

It seems as a part of his enhancement of the crystal set he had attached the aerial to the telephone hook-up, with the result that mother had no doubt been party to a conversation between her neighbour, who was on the same party line, and some other person whose responses to the information imparted obviously duplicated mother's.

More than fifty years later I had a similar experience, one that has yet to be explained. I woke up one night to the sound of a heavily accented voice saying,

"Jackie ... Where's Jackie."

There was a terrible urgency in the voice. I knew I wasn't dreaming but I couldn't imagine where this voice was coming from. Knowing that my friend Jackie Webster would not think me insane, I called her and passed on the message; that a woman with a deep voice and a thick European accent, had called me out of my sleep in the middle of the night looking for her.

"I do believe I know who it is," she said.

Later she told me that it was a Hungarian refugee who was trying to contact her but didn't know she was living in Fredericton. The woman knew we were friends and thought that maybe I could help her find Jackie.

My sister, Pat McLeod who makes her home in Fredericton now, is also a believer. She particularly enjoys sharing the story of how, when she was living in St. Stephen, half-an-hour after he died our father stopped by for coffee with her and her neighbour, Mrs. Getchell.

Some of the stories in this book involve forerunners. Such as the time when I was driving home to Hampton from Saint John one afternoon around three-thirty.

I slowed down to make the turn onto the humpback railway bridge near our house as the train we called 'the jitney' (a small electric train) went under it. What I saw coming out the other side was an old-fashioned, black steam engine with a big bundle of clothing on the 'cowcatcher'. (An iron grill in the shape of a huge scoop attached to the front of the engine. Stray cows wandering the tracks frequently ended up there).

The vision was only a flash before I was on the bridge. I chided myself for my silly imagination.

That night when I sat down at five o'clock to watch the television news the lead story was about a man walking the railway track, being hit by a train and killed. The train was the jitney I had seen coming under the bridge but which my imagination pictured as a steam engine with a large bundle of clothing on the cowcatcher. The vision occurred about twenty minutes before the man was killed.

Sometimes with forerunners it is possible to tie them to an event, other times it's not. To my knowledge forerunners never do give one the opportunity to change an event.

My daughter Barbara's experience was not a forerunner, it was more of a forewarning. One that saved her life.

Barbie taught ballet on Prince Edward Island for a number of years and one night when she was driving home to Summerside, tired yet stimulated from a dance workshop in Charlottetown, she stopped suddenly and pulled off to the side of the road.

"It was really strange," she said. "One minute my mind was going full tilt over the day's happenings then next it was as if an operator broke in on a telephone call and said 'pull off the road right now.' Yet nothing was verbalized, I was just commanded to do it. In the same instant, again without verbalizing, I was assured that nothing had happened to my children.

"Within an instant I was given permission to go on again. The whole experience might have taken two minutes in all but I feel it was less than one minute.

"I was travelling a road that intersected with the main highway and, shortly after I pulled out, I came to the intersection and stopped. Just as I did a big black car with no lights on came barrelling down the highway on the wrong side of the road!

"If I had not pulled off the road for whatever time it was I would have been halfway across that highway when that car came along."

Although Barbie was shaken she was also curious. Something or someone had reached into her subconscious and made her stop the car. It happened a short time after her grandmother died and her conclusion was that Hooey's (my children's affectionate name for their grandmother Ryder) spirit was still around at the time, and still watching over her.

"It was a wonderfully comforting feeling," she said.

People ask me if my house is haunted and I have to say 'yes', but then I have to qualify that answer because I really don't know what is going on in my house ... on the other side of the curtain.

The night of the August day in 1962 when we moved into our Hampton home I went to bed too tired to sleep. I lay there for the longest time, my head buzzing. Then I got this strange feeling. It was more than a sense of being watched, it was a feeling that 'we', as a family, were being sized up. Examined.

I was too tired to care and dropped off to sleep with the feeling that 'whatever would be, would be'.

I awoke the next morning with an instant sense of wellbeing. Later I told Fred, my husband, that I felt we had passed some kind of test. That the house had accepted us.

He looked sceptical.

From that time forward I have always felt at ease in my home, for all its rambling size and history.

Others have not. My youngest daughter, Cindy, maintains to this day that a ghost lives in the closet of her old bedroom. She says he wears a long, old-fashioned army greatcoat, nipped in at the waist like that of an officer's.

There could be some justification for this. The owner of our house before we bought it from his estate, was a

Colonel Ryder. Both he and his wife died at home after living quiet but industrious post- Second World War lives on the property.

Possibly the blame for our hauntings rests with my sister and me for inviting strange ghosts to move in.

Across the road from us is what is still known as the 'Ryan Castle' property, built by a dentist who used industrial diamonds to fill the teeth of royalty in his Paris office at the turn of the century. Once a landmark in Hampton all that remains of it is a crumbling concrete basement.

According to a story told me by the late Sadie Folkins and corroborated by the late Walter Mitton, both of whom worked there, the castle was haunted by a rather belligerent ghost who, whenever something displeased her, regularly stormed through the place slamming open doors and throwing around the knives that had been used, unsuccessfully, to keep them closed.

At the time the castle burned down and the next year, when the stable met the same fate, my sister and I were sitting on the front terrace watching the spectacle. We were talking about the castle's history and feeling sad for the poor ghosts who would now have no place to haunt.

"I suppose they could always come here," I offered. "After all they were friends of my ghosts back in the old days."

"Why don't you invite them over then?" Pat said.

"Consider it done," I replied.

That night there was a bat in my house. The first time to my knowledge one had ever come in. We decided that it must have brought the ghost of Dr. Ryan over and thought no more of it. The following year when the stables burned the same thing occurred, for only the second time in the more than thirty years we have lived in this house, a bat came in and was never seen again. We joked at the time about who might have been haunting the stables all those years.

My daughter-in-law didn't think it was a joke when she was staying here one time. Every time she took a shower or a bath she could sense someone leering at her!

Well, Dr. Ryan was said to be a bit of a lady's man in his day. Who knows, maybe he arrived here on the wings of a bat back in the 1960s?

But enough of me and mine. Let's read the wonderful stories of other New Brunswickers who have shared their lives with ghosts, demons or other spirits from beyond the pale. ༐

His grandfather's clock will never chime again

When Charles (Mousie) Flanagan's grandfather, John Flanagan, emigrated from Ireland, he brought an old wooden clock to Fredericton with him. According to Mousie it wasn't anything very fancy but if it didn't have an eerie history before coming to Fredericton it created one there for the Flanagan family.

Here is Mousie's story as he told it to me. ꝺꝺ

My grandfather's clock was just an old-fashioned mantel clock made of dark wood, it could have been either mahogany or walnut. The top was curved and a bit of decorative wainscotting flared out from the sides of the square base.

The only thing that was unusual about it is that no one could remember if the clock ever worked, at least it never worked in my memory or that of my father. The family kept it on the mantel anyway because it was an heirloom, after all.

The strange thing is that the clock did gong or chime on rare occasions, *very* rare occasions.

There is no record of it having struck when my grandfather died but, on April 24, 1928, my father ... he was Frank Flanagan ... heard it strike in the middle of the night.

The next morning they wondered where Uncle Tom, my grandfather's brother, was. They found him dead in his bed.

The family was living at the time in a house at 222 St. John Street.The house is still standing. Two weeks after Uncle Tom died my mother died, on May 8, 1928 and the same thing happened. The old clock that had never worked, struck, or kept time at all chimed again in the middle of the night. The next morning my mother was found dead.

Now that, in itself, is strange enough but it's not the end of the story. We moved from St. John Street to 229 Aberdeen Street and, in June, 1937 ... I'm not entirely sure of the day, the clock struck once again and that time I heard it. It was a loud chime, guaranteed to wake you up.

It was the middle of the night again, everyone was in bed asleep and the clock had only ever struck twice before to anyone's knowledge. The next morning our live-in housekeeper wasn't up when we came down to breakfast. When we went to check on her we found her dead in her room.

Well, my father went into a rage.

"That son-of-a-bitch-of-a-clock will never strike for anyone again!" he said.

He took that clock off the mantle and out to the woodshed then he picked up the axe and he smashed it to bits. Not content with that he burned the wood and then trashed the metal workings beyond recognition. Then he sent what was left to the dump.

To tell you the truth we were all glad that old clock was gone. ꙮ

He said he was sorry
for our grief
... but we
weren't
grieving!

Ferne Coughlan of Nashwaak Bridge was always intrigued by the story her grandmother used to tell of the peddler with the gift of precognition. Her daughter, Patricia A. Quent of Fleume Ridge, heard the author on the Fredericton CBC station asking for stories during an interview and kindly sent off an outline. Here is the story as told by Mrs. Coughlan. ➤➤

It was always said in our family that my grandmother, who we called *Aunt Fanny* for some unknown reason, was prone to have premonitions from time-to-time. Be that as it may, in this story I believe it was the peddler who had that gift.

Fanny Fraser was the youngest of the large family of Thomas Fraser, a shoemaker in Nashwaak Bridge. Her mother had died in childbirth in 1860. Fanny was twenty-two years old at the time of this story, and had not yet married my grandfather, Malcolm McCrae.

Some of the other girls in the family were also home the day they noticed a peddler standing by the gate. He stood there for fifteen or twenty minutes before coming up to the house. When he got there he told the girls he was sorry to intrude on their grief but he was very hungry and wondered if they would be kind enough to give him something to eat.

They hastened to prepare him a lunch of cold meat, possibly some preserves, and a cup of tea. When he sat down to eat they asked him what he meant by saying he was *sorry for intruding on their grief.*

He explained that he had been waiting at the gate for the funeral procession to leave. He then went on to describe the funeral in detail, even to speaking of an old lady's horse rearing up and acting so badly that it had to be led from the procession.

My grandmother said they didn't think much of it at the time until their father died a few weeks later. Everything happened the day of the funeral exactly the way the peddler had described it.

Even to the horse rearing up! My grandmother said that the horse belonged to Meg Urquhart.

Our home is nearby the remains of the fireplace, all that's left of the old family home that burned a few years back. I always sort of expected that someday I might see something there come out of the past but so far as I know, no one has seen that peddler or any other such presence near the site. ᵥᵥ

Debbie fought off the demons she courted in the Sixties

My daughter Barbara told me about a woman she knew when she lived in Fredericton. She said the woman had a lot of problems with demons, so much so that she had to have her home exorcised. The woman's first name was Debbie and she worked at the daycare my granddaughter Bianca attended. She and Debbie's daughter Cindy had been five-year-old bosom buddies.

Luck was on my side. I located the daycare where Debbie had worked fifteen years ago and learned where Debbie lived. When I telephoned her my call was answered by a young person who confirmed that she was Cindy.

I was not prepared for the reaction when I introduced myself as Bianca's grandmother. A high-pitched shriek nearly shattered my eardrum then there was a crash as the telephone dropped to a tabletop or the floor. The words 'Mom! You won't believe this...' faded into the distance before I could say a word about why I was calling, or ask to speak to her mother.

A short time later a breathless Cindy explained that, no more than an hour before my call, she and her mother had been watching the Oprah Winfrey Show on which the question, 'If you could meet and talk to one person you hadn't seen for a long time, who would you most like it to be?' was under discussion.

"I turned to Mom and said, 'I would really like to see Bianca again. Remember my friend at daycare?"

I gave Cindy Bianca's address and telephone number and she immediately called her. A short time later Bianca came for a visit and the two girls got together for an evening of memories and renewed friendship.

Because of the nature of the story that Cindy's mother tells here, I have agreed to respect her request for privacy.

"It's a part of our life that is finally behind us," Debbie said, "and I don't ever want to bring it back." ∂∂

A child of the Sixties

I was a child of the sixties and of all that term implies; not just the music, although that was a part of it, but the drugs and the booze, voodooism and devil worship, experimenting with new things all the time. Cards, spells, trances, everything. Our lives were centred on getting a 'high' by whatever means it took.

We had reached a point where the ouija board was running our lives and, in September of 1977 my husband and I became suddenly frightened by what we were doing, and had done. We were beginning to get answers that we didn't like and we were frightened but didn't know where to go for help.

Satan was in control.

It was around this time that I began to look at this friend of ours who seemed to have it all together. He was a religious man and he used to preach at us but he also seemed to live what he preached. He projected this sense of peace. Every Sunday he drove twenty miles to pick up Cindy, she was four at the time, and take her to Sunday School. After that he took her to his home for lunch before bringing her back again in the afternoon.

As I said, my husband and I were open to anything new. We had never tried church before, although I was brought up to go to church as a child. One Sunday we decided there must be something to it that we were missing, since Bill seemed to have everything together so well.

We went off to church, giggling and prepared to sit there and laugh and nudge each other throughout the service. We were ready to poke fun at everything that went on.

I was sitting there in the pew, hearing the minister say the same old things that ministers always say but this time I was hearing something else in the words. Something different was going on.

The next thing I knew I was standing up in front of the altar. Now I am the kind of person who would never, never put on a public display. It wouldn't matter what happened to me I wouldn't cry in public, I don't get angry in public ... I keep everything to myself.

So here I am standing in front of the altar and this voice inside my head is saying, "This is where you need to be."

We went home that day bewildered.

I had gone forward and I couldn't believe that I had done that. My husband said he wanted to go forward too but he was too proud to let himself do it.

So he said to me, "I don't think we better go back. We kind of made fools of ourselves, what with you going forward and everything and us being the kind of people we are."

The next day I was sweeping the floor, doing my regular housework. I was in the sun room, dusting the plants hanging from the ceiling and I started talking.

"What do you think, Lord? These plants don't look too good, maybe I should give them some plant food."

All of a sudden I realized I was standing there talking to God and I thought, "I'm flipping out!"

I never let my husband know about it but I kept doing it more and more often until finally I told Bill, who was Cindy's Godfather, and he said, "Let me give you a book to read."

It was called *The Way.*

I sat down and read it all the way through. I was fascinated.

I had heard all the stories before but they seemed different.

By this time I had been off drugs for a few years. I gave them up right away when I found I was pregnant with Cindy, I was afraid they might do some harm to my baby. So by now both my husband and I were pretty clean although we still had our cards and the ouija board and all the other trappings of the devil worship we were into.

After reading that book I decided that I was going to give my heart to the Lord, and I did. It was three months before my husband did, he was afraid God was going to take everything that he enjoyed away from him, including his precious Corvette.

Almost from the day that I decided I would have nothing to do with Satan I became sick. I was so sick that I was constantly vomiting and I was afraid all the time.

Although we had started to go to church I couldn't bring myself to go anymore because I felt so terrible. Finally, one night when Bill and a friend of his came up to visit I told them about how I felt and of the terrible fear I had in my heart.

They said, "That's Satan trying to keep you to himself."

I thought that was nothing but a lot of Mumbo-Jumbo. I just laughed at them, I had visions of someone saying "I just *love* the Lord" ... and turning out to be Jimmy Swaggart.

The truth was I was dragging my feet. My husband still hadn't made a commitment and we still had all our old spell books and ouija board in the house.

The turning point for me came one morning when I woke up with a start to what sounded like a twenty-piece band playing in the living room. I thought to myself, *What is going on?* The kids were too small to be the cause of it, besides it was still too early in the morning for them to be getting up.

I got out of bed and went into the living-room and the racket stopped.

I thought I must have been dreaming. I went back to bed and back to sleep.

The next thing I knew I heard someone calling me. "Debbie! Debbie!"

I looked up and these beaded, hippie-style curtains I had hanging on the door started swaying and I thought I was tripping out. I wondered if maybe my husband had done something, or given something to me because he didn't want to quit and wanted to get me back on drugs. But I knew in my heart he wasn't that kind of person.

So I got up and I called Bill and his friend and told them what was happening and they came out to the house. I'll never forget that day as long as I live.

I said to them, "How am I going to get Satan out of my life?"

They said I had to start by getting rid of everything in the house that related to Satan. All the books, the ouija boards, the cards. Everything. Not only that but I had to do it myself and I had to burn them myself. No one else could do it for me.

I took the posters down off the wall, I even got rid of playing cards although they are harmless. I wasn't taking any chances.

But when I tried to burn them they wouldn't burn. I lit the fire and I lit the fire and I lit the fire … and they would not burn. It was all paper and a ouija board made of wood, for heaven's sake!

Well, my husband came home and he said, "I'll make it burn!" I knew then that he had made his commitment to the Lord too.

He went down to the basement and got some kerosene or something and it finally started to burn. I thought for sure it would go Boom! and practically explode but it didn't. It just burned very slowly.

We started trying to live a Christian family life but all hell broke out in the house. Literally.

Our friends didn't want to come visit because it was so cold they couldn't sit in our home, we could see their breath, even with the fireplace on. We weren't cold, they were.

We also started having manifestations in the house. It wasn't just my husband and I, it was our children too. Even to this day every once in awhile Cindy will see a man in a black rain coat and black hat standing at the foot of the stairs.

The whole thing sort of ended with a real climax one day when my son, still a baby in diapers, was upstairs in his bed. I was downstairs reading my Bible and when I put it down on the coffee table to go do something else he started screaming, then Cindy came running downstairs yelling, "Mommy! Mommy! Come quick! There's a man in Jimmy's room!"

I ran upstairs and Jimmy was standing in his crib and it was shaking fit to break, there was a white shag carpet in his room and it was pulsating under the crib. He was terrified.

I grabbed him out of the crib and I grabbed Cindy by the hair to drag her away, she was standing there frozen.

"Look Mommy," she said, "that man is laughing at you!"

There wasn't anyone there that I could see.

"What is it? What man?"

"That man," she said, "he's laughing at you! He's laughing at you!"

"Who is it?" I said.

"He says his name is Satan," she told me.

At that point I decided that either I was losing it or my children were losing it or something was totally out of control, and I was some scared. As I ran past one of the rooms on the way downstairs the drawers were opening and closing and the bathroom door was banging open and shut and Jimmy and Cindy were screaming at the top of their lungs.

Once downstairs I collapsed on the sofa and I was shaking so bad I couldn't control myself but for some unknown reason I reached out and I opened the Bible.

The second I opened it everything stopped. There was like a roar in the house, then silence.

I grabbed the telephone to get help. I was holding Jimmy in one arm, Cindy was hanging on to the other one and I was holding onto the Bible and trying to dial the phone at the same time.

Finally I got through to the pastor and I said, "Dick, I need help!"

He said, "Yes. I know. John is here with me and we were praying when we suddenly had an overwhelming feeling that we should come to your house."

I said "Please, come right now!"

As soon as I said that there was another roar, like a monster screaming.

I started reading 'The Lord is my shepherd, I shall not want ...' and I just kept reading and reading from the Bible.

And the house got so quiet it was eerie. When that happened I suddenly got mad. I was raging mad. I put the kids down on the couch and I started screaming.

"Who do you think you are to do this to me and my family?"

I held up the Bible and I started reading out of it at the top of my lungs and I went all through the house doing that. Just screaming. I sounded like some way-out Bible-thumper but I didn't care. I was mad.

The pastor arrived and I called my husband and he came home without my even telling him what was going on.

The pastor said he wasn't sure how much he could believe of what I was telling him but he would go through every room in that house reading from the Bible and putting the sign of the cross on every door, because that's what the Bible said for him to do.

After that things settled down. But for awhile I was angry with God and with the church because life became very difficult for me and my family and I felt we weren't getting the support we needed.

I stuck with my Bible though, even if I didn't stick with the church and now life is going on at a more even keel.

I don't answer to anybody anymore, except to God.

To this day I have neighbours who still believe that I practice Satanism. ৯৯

The Haunted Hangar
and Other Stories

Marlene Abbot and her husband, Mark Richards operate a graphic design business in the Wayside Industries building, where members of his family have worked for half a century. Once an airplane hangar, the building remains little changed from its days of fame when it was Saint John's Millidgeville Airport.

Some of the stories Marlene and Mark have shared with me involve this historic building. Others are primarily Marlene's stories, revealing a highly sensitive personality who has inherited her second sight from equally sensitive parents.

Of the two stories involving Wayside Industries Marlene was present for only one experience.

In the days when transAtlantic flights were making aviation history the City of Saint John's bustling Millidgeville Airport was once a favourite stop-off place for such famous pilots as Amelia Earhart. It served the community well from the time it was established, in 1928, until 1952 when the present airport was opened.

Today, it is difficult to imagine that the upscale suburban Millidgeville area of Saint John was once an isolated, rural community. It is even more difficult to realize that the large, almost windowless building nestled among the houses is an aeroplane hangar that once housed the feisty little double-winged aircraft that Mark Richards' father can remember from his childhood.

For nearly 25 years that hangar has been home to a specialized printing company, Wayside Industries.

In the mind of Mark Richards there is no question of there being a ghost and no question but that the ghost is a man, not only has Mark heard him but both he and Marlene have seen him. ▸▸

The Haunted Hangar

I used to work at the warehouse at night when I was in high school, I think it was around 1987.

When I worked the night shift we started after five-thirty in the evening and worked as late as around three-thirty in the morning. There were about seven of us on the crew, myself and one of the women operated a printing press and I was also responsible for cleaning up after the shift. That usually took about forty-five minutes after the run was done. Because I'm competitive, I guess, I would work right up until the end of the shift in order to get a better production record for the evening crew before I began the cleanup.

I'd be alone here at the factory until about quarter after four and that was fine. I had no problem with it. I just lived around the corner so it was only a five-minute walk home ... less than that if you're running, I discovered!

This particular night everything was going fine. I had cleaned up the press and, because I was the last one finished, it was my responsibility to make the rounds. I had to make sure the door was locked and that all the lights were off.

I went through the main plant, shutting down the six or seven light switches and panels in there and then I came to the alleyway. It's about ten feet long and ten feet wide and leads to the secondary warehouse where the loading dock is. I used it as an exit at night because I didn't have a key and the loading door automatically locks when you pull it down from outside.

I turned the last of the lights off in the alleyway then I walked around the outside of this big dumpster and reached in behind it and pulled the chain to close the automatic door. The door started to close so I ducked underneath it to the outside, but it wouldn't come down all the way. It would only come down as far as waist high. I tugged and pounded but it wouldn't budge.

I thought 'Oh, that's great! Someone's piled up some skids beside the door and now I can't close it.' I reached inside and I could feel some two-by-fours there so I pushed them out of the way and managed to get the door down as far as my knees, but it wouldn't go down any farther.

By then I was getting really frustrated. I was tired and it was late and I didn't want to go back in there and turn on all those lights again and try and figure out what was going on.

I just wanted to go home.

Anyway, I put the door back up and went back in, intending to walk around the dumpster again and into the warehouse to the light panel. It was pitch black in there, you couldn't see your hand in front of your face.

I could hear the wind whistling around in the old hangar, it always creaks and groans and makes a lot of strange noises, things shift and set-tle constantly but the night noises never meant much to me. My family's association with the plant goes back a long way, which probably accounts for why I feel so comfortable there.

My grandfather was custodian when the plant was an airplane hangar and lots of nights, when my father and his friends were around twelve or thirteen years old, they would come in here and play . They would get in the old biplanes, start them up and race them around the hangar.

I grew up hearing stories about the place so the ghostly noises never bothered me. They just go with the plant, naturally.

On that particular night I had walked half-way to the the alleyway when I heard the sound of a man's footsteps coming towards me. They must have been thirty or forty feet away from me. I could tell they were coming into the alleyway because it's a smaller area and things sound tinnier than in the plant where there are forty and fifty foot high ceilings.

So I called out. I thought there must have been someone else still there that I didn't know about, so I called out to them.

Nobody answered.

I said to myself, 'Geez! What's going on here?'

The first thing I thought of was that it was

my brother. He was, and still is, the manager of Wayside Industries, and he often comes in to do some work at night. Sometimes if I was working here and didn't know he had come in, he'd sneak up behind me and try to scare me. So naturally, the first thing I thought of when I heard those footsteps was that it was Guy, pulling one of his tricks.

I called out, 'Guy! Is that you? Stop trying to scare me ... you better look out. I've got a stick here!'

Well, there was no other sound, just the footsteps coming towards me.

'I'm not kidding, Guy ... or whoever it is! I can't see a thing and if you come any closer I'm going to hit you with this stick!'

Not a thing. Not a word. Just the footsteps coming closer and closer. So I picked up a piece of wood by the dumpster and I threw it.

Then I ran.

I scrambled under the door and didn't stop until I was into the light out there in the yard.

Well, I sat there and I waited. And I waited. But there was nothing, no one. Finally I went home to bed.

The next morning my brother gave me a hard time about not locking up but I didn't tell him what happened. Not then, at least.

I did tell a few people that I heard someone and I asked different ones if it was them but nobody said anything. I wouldn't have been surprised at someone playing a joke on me but no one ever confessed to it to this day ... and I think they would have eventually. That's part of the fun of it.

I do know that over the years the men who have worked at Wayside Industries have had their own stories to relate about the old airplane hangar.

Marlene and Mark were working together in the plant one night when the following experience left no doubt in their minds but that there was, indeed a ghost at Wayside Industries. ◊◊

In the summer of 1988 Mark and Marlene were working on a piece of equipment called a 'waxer' when

*Well, am I
doing it right?*

they both began to get the feeling they were being
watched.

"I was putting the paper stock in the machine at
one end and Marlene was taking it off, fifteen feet away,
at the other end and putting it in a skid (a small plat-
form where material can be stored or moved around).
We were actually facing each other from each end of the
waxer but I had the feeling that someone else besides
Marlene was watching me."

"I couldn't get over the feeling that someone was
watching me, someone other than Mark. Yet we were the
only ones there. Still, I couldn't keep myself from constantly looking up the hall between the big printers."

"I kept telling myself, 'This is ridiculous!' but the
feeling wouldn't go away. Then, at one point I turned
right around for some reason and there he was, between

the printer and the cutter!

" 'Aha,' I thought, 'I've caught you!'

"He wasn't a very big man. I'm about five feet seven inches tall and the man wasn't any taller than I am, maybe shorter. But there he was, standing there. He was wearing a light coloured shirt, green work pants with his hands in the pockets and wearing rubber boots, like hip waders rolled down. I couldn't see the face very well.

"I just stood there and stared. Then I said, 'Well, am I doing it right?' And 'Poof'. He disappeared."

The sensation of being watched went with him. Marlene neither sensed him nor saw him again.

"The place where Marlene saw the figure of a man was the same place that the footstep started from the night I had been frightened. The night when I thought I heard someone walking from the plant and down the alleyway to the loading dock.

"After we finished work that night I asked Marlene if she had felt anything strange in the plant, I knew that on other occasions and in other places she had sensed and seen unexplained presences.

"When she told me what happened I said that I, too, had sensed someone watching me.

"I had looked up several times but I didn't see anything, then one time I got a glimpse of something about twenty feet away. All I saw was a shirt and pants but mostly it was a yellow glow. An aura? I don't know.

"I noticed that Marlene was acting a little funny down at the end of the machine but I didn't say anything to her until after we finished work and left.

"We agree that what we saw seemed to be illuminated, mostly from the waist up as far as I was concerned although Marlene could more clearly see the clothing and the boots because she was within ten feet of the figure.

"It was a soft, sunny yellow glow. More radiant than anything else. A head, but no face. But it was definitely a man.

"From what I know of the late Bert Newell, the man who established Wayside Industries, the figure does not resemble him ... and Mr. Newell invariably wore a business suit.

"Could it have been a pilot of an earlier age? Possibly, but would hip-wader type rubber boots have been a natural kind of footgear?"

"One thing is certain," Marlene says, "is that if anything or anyone is here from another dimension or another world it is benign. There is no sense whatever of anything evil or with evil intentions.

"What I get more than anything else is a feeling of curiosity. As if we are being observed."

Mark came back to the plant the next night and spent about fifteen minutes "just talking" to whoever or whatever it was.

"I was challenging it, I guess. I said things like 'Why did you try to scare us last night?' 'Why don't you come out and show yourself?'

"I walked through the whole plant saying things like that but nothing happened. I don't know if anyone was listening or not.

"I didn't get any response at all." ♊

You're afraid of the stove, I said ... and Poof! she disappeared

Marlene not only experienced but she saw the friendly spirit that haunted the older, salt box-style house on West Street in Halifax where she and husband Mark were living while studying at the Nova Scotia College of Art and Design.

It was a woman, a little old lady. I knew it was a woman from the beginning when I first began to get the feeling of being followed around the house. I knew right away there was a presence in the house, it wasn't the first time and it wouldn't be the last time that I sensed someone or something in a parallel space.

There were no bad feelings in the house, I was just a little annoyed at being followed all the time. She was one more very curious presence in my life and I really wanted to find out what she was all about.

I used to catch her in a little hallway. You came up from downstairs in the basement to an odd doorway that opened into the kitchen but with the hallway right next to it and then another doorway into the living room on the other side. I would come up from the basement and there would be a *whoosh* of air and I could tell she had been watching me come up the stairs and had scooted past and into the hall for fear I would see her.

I could tell she was little. I'm quite tall for a woman but she was only up to my shoulder at the most, because the *whoosh* of air didn't come up very high.

Then finally I caught her. I was in the kitchen one day, standing at the stove, and I turned around quickly to reach for something ... and there she was! A little old lady sort of hunched up into herself. She had a house dress on and she was kind of looking at me with her head to one side but I realized she wasn't really looking at me, she was looking at the stove.

It was a propane stove and she seemed to be looking at the pilot light. I had never had a propane stove before and I used to worry about it a lot for that reason. One day I came home and the pilot light was out and I was petrified.

Anyway, she was not looking at me, she was looking through me because I was in front of the stove and she had a frightened expression on her face.

'You're afraid of the stove!' I said.

As soon as I spoke she disappeared. *Poof!* Just like that and I didn't see her again, but I knew she was still there.

One time I got a bad case of the flu and I was throwing up all the time. I was so sick I finally had to go to the clinic and get a gravol shot.

I crawled into bed as soon as I got home and as I lay there I knew I was being watched, all day long, and I didn't mind. It was actually comforting. I was so sick it felt good to know I was being watched over. I could sense her hovering around the foot of the bed and around the doorway.

I missed her when we moved away. ৯৯

It was a long casket and I couldn't understand why: My grandmother was only four feet, eleven inches tall!

When Marlene first started having dreams about people dying, dreams that often started three days before someone she knew died and ran every night like a soap opera, she said it was "a really awful feeling ... because although I do have those three days to figure out just who it is that is going to die I never know who until they are dead."

Here are two of those stories. ঌঌ

The dreams always start out like a hum in my head and then there's a *Snap!* or a *Click!* or a *Buzz!* and there it is.

It's like a camera starting to roll and it keeps rolling for three nights, each time taking me a little further toward learning who it is that will die.

In my dream I see myself in places that I can't, at first, understand why I am there.

The first time it happened I was away at university and I dreamed I had to go home for a funeral. In my dream I thought, 'Oh, the only one I know of who could be near death would be my grandmother.' She was nearly eighty years old at the time. I remember dreaming that it was logical ... until as the dream continued I discovered I was in the Baptist church in Chance Harbour, and I had never been in that church before in my life.

Still in my dream I looked down the aisle and I could see this very long coffin and I thought, 'That's strange. My grandmother is only four feet eleven inches tall!'

Besides, what would a good Catholic like her be doing in a Baptist church?

The next morning I remembered the dream and I was really upset so I called my parents, my father is a fisherman in Chance Harbour, just to make sure my grandmother hadn't died, and she hadn't.

The next night my dream took me a little bit further down the aisle of the church and I could see that all the people there were fishermen. 'Oh! Oh!' I told myself, 'something has happened to one of the fishermen.'

The next day I was home from classes early. It was 1985 and I can remember it so clearly. I caught the news on the television and they were saying a boat had gone down off Mahogany Island.

Mom called right after that and said, 'Marlene, I want you to know it wasn't your father.'

"I know," I said. And I did know, somehow, it wasn't my father. But I still didn't know *who* it was.

That night in my dream I got up as far as the casket and this woman was there beside it and she was crying. As soon as I saw her I knew who it was that had drowned.

Mom called the next morning and said, 'I just called to let you know who it was …

"I know," I said. "It was John Mawhinney."

"How did you know that?" she asked. "Has it been on the news already?"

No, I said. And I told her about the dream. I had recognized his mother, of course.

It seems the boats were coming down the bay with their lobster traps when a freak wave came up and broke the gunwales and swamped the boat John and his brother were on and they were washed overboard. It happened so fast they didn't have time to get the dingy off. All the boys had was some flotsam to cling to. One of them survived the other one, the younger one, John … the tall one … didn't.

The second time the same sort of thing happened was the following February. I dreamed an old friend, Arthur Belding … we were born on the same day … and I were walking along the beach . He was wearing a Joe Cocker style maroon-colored shirt, jeans, and hip rubber boots. We were reading the names on a monument to the local people who had died at sea.

"This is wrong," I said to my friend, "John's name isn't there, they put down Mark's name by mistake."

Mark Mawhinney is the brother who survived the boat accident.

The next night the same thing … *Click! Buzz!* and

my dream rolled on to this picture. I was back on the beach, looking at the monument and I turned around and started to say the same thing again, that the wrong name was there ... but Arthur was gone!

The next morning my mother called.

"I have some sad news for you," she said.

"I know," I said. "Arthur Belding died."

"How did you know?" she asked me. I told her that he disappeared in my dream.

Arthur's wife was in the hospital and he got a call to say his daughter was being born. It was late when the boat came in, two o'clock in the morning, and he just got in the car and started out for the hospital right away. But he fell asleep driving on the highway and hit the abutment at the Powerhouse Road. The car turned over and landed upside down in the creek. Arthur was knocked out and when the tide came in he drowned.

I was very upset about these things for a long time. Then I talked to my father about what was happening to me. Not just about the dreams but about the ghosts and all the strange things that seemed to be going on around me.

"You just have to accept it," he said. "I did, a long time ago. You get it from both your mother and me. All I can tell you is to accept it."

And I did, eventually. ♪♪

Flowers for Marion

This is one of those stories the reader will have to accept my word for because the narrator, whose name is Bill, is concerned for the family that owns the house he rents. He doesn't feel he has the right to expose them to public scrutiny.

"If they want to talk about their house and the spirit that inhabits it, that's fine. All I am telling you is my story, my experience while living here."

At the time we talked he was hoping to develop a business and settle in Saint John on a permanent basis. In the meantime he had rented a house in West Saint John, a house that the former tenants insisted was haunted.

I interviewed him in that house and, following my taping, I was given a tour from basement to attic. I asked him to allow me to sense for myself, if I could, where the spirit he calls 'Marion' defined her presence the strongest.

We were almost at the centre of the upper hall when I walked into a space that was icy cold.

"Is this her place?" I asked. I was facing a very large but very ordinary wardrobe.

"Yes," he said, opening the wardrobe door. "This is where she kept her treasures. This is where I found the picture of her standing nude by the waterfall."

He reached in and brought out an old, hand-tinted photograph of a nude woman beside a waterfall, taken perhaps in the 1920s or 1930s.

"But she's lovely!" I said.

"Yes, but I think she's ashamed of the photograph, because she hid it behind here, taped to the back of the wardrobe."

Without thinking, I spoke directly to the presence I could sense near me. "You have nothing to be ashamed of in this photograph." I said. "You were a lovely woman. This is a wonderful memento of your youth."

Almost instantly as we stood there talking, the space that had been icy cold assumed the same moderate temperature of the rest of the house.

She was gone, at least for the time being.

Here is Bill's story. ৯৯

I was talking to a couple of people where I was doing some work, I said I was tired of staying in hotels. Since I planned to stick around Saint John I said I wanted something more permanent.

One of the men told me he and his girl friend were moving out of a place, maybe I would like to look at it.

I said, 'Okay' and I came out here and looked around. It's not the most comfortably built house for today's living. The sitting room is small, it's not arranged in a way that makes it easy to watch television and it was never intended as a place to entertain more than maybe two people at a time, but I thought it would do for the time being and I told them that.

Well, they sort of looked at each other and he said, "I have to tell you something before you finally decide."

He said the place was all right but that he and his girl friend were leaving because they couldn't stand the ghost.

Being a nonbeliever myself I just brushed it off and said, "That won't bother me."

He went on to tell me they even had a psychic come in to see if they could find out what was happening, and why. The person they got said there were no demons or evil spirits, nothing like that. She told them it was just a restless spirit.

Restless spirit or not, they could only stand it for a few months and they decided to move out. The place, he said, was still available if I wanted it.

I told them, 'Hey, I don't believe in ghosts ...'

At least I didn't.

I came over and did a lot of cleaning and fixed the place up a bit and, outside of being cluttered and not very clean, I couldn't see what they were complaining about.

Once I moved in, it was a different story.

First, there were a lot a noises I couldn't identify

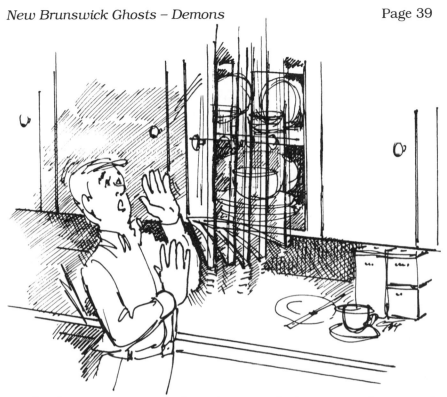

in the beginning and objects were being moved around,
I'd be sure I put something one place and it would end
up in another and there was no one in that house except
me. I can state that for a fact because there's an alarm
system and I keep it turned on.

For the first ten days I had very little of my own
stuff. There was no stereo equipment here, for example.
So all I had was a little tape recorder thing and I would
put it here, on the dining room table, with a tape in it
and I would go across the hall to the bathroom or whatever and the sound would start fluctuating. It would get
real low, so I could hardly hear it, then another time it
would blare so loud it was unbearable.

One day when this happened I was out in the
kitchen and I came to the door between the dining room
and the kitchen and I said, jokingly, "Stop that fooling
around with my tape deck!"

All hell broke loose! The cabinet doors in the wall
nearest me started banging ... open and shut, open and
shut ... right past my head.

Well-l-l-l.

That was when I began to wonder if I had been wrong about ghosts.

There is no way that cabinet door could have slammed back and forth like that on its own. Someone or something had to be doing it. There had to be a reason for it.

Then one night as I was walking upstairs I identified one of the sounds I kept hearing. It was a sound like oxygen flowing, like you can hear in a hospital.

By this time I had asked some questions of people, like the man who was doing some work on the kitchen counters. He had been a pall bearer at the funeral of the woman who had always lived in the house, her name was Marion, he said. Apparently there was friction of some kind in the family and, while I don't know exactly when she died I know it was some time ago and I do think it is a bit strange that all of her things are still here in the house. Very personal things.

Her son said that she died here in the house and that her death had been a very painful and long, drawn-out one. She was very sick for a long time before she died and had to be watched carefully because she was always choking.

Eventually she was confined to bed upstairs most of the time. During the day nurses came in and cared for her and, at night, her husband was there to make sure she was all right.

Sometimes, in the middle of the night, I wake up and I hear coughing, I really do, and it's not me coughing in my sleep because I still hear it after I wake up.

Other times I'll hear footsteps, it could be day or night, and I find strange things in strange places. One earring on the side of the bathroom sink ... it's not mine and I live here alone.

Silly little things are left on the dining room table, items like picture hooks, tacks and they're all grubby and well-used. One day I came home and found a small brass dinner bell beside the sink. I had never seen it before, but suddenly it was there. It's probably the biggest of the items I have found.

I generally keep my counters very clean so I notice

when silly small things like that appear on them, one at a time.

I've never actually seen anything move ... but things do move.

I'll put something on my desk and it will move to the table. Or I'll put something on the table and it will appear on my desk.

One day I took the vacuum out to do some cleaning and I put it in the corner because something on the television caught my attention and I sat down to watch. Later on I went out to the kitchen and started to get some lunch and the vacuum cleaner started going in the front room, all by itself.

I just said "Stop it" and she did.

It was this kind of thing that made the other guy move out. He said one time the bathroom door closed and locked from the inside and there was no one in there. They had to take the door off the hinges to get in.

I admit that after the first week I was having second thoughts about staying. Too many things were happening. Then, quite by accident, I discovered the secret of coexistence with my ghost.

I spent a lot of my life working in Europe and, over there, you tend to get into the habit of buying flowers. It's part of the way of life. I got so one of the first things I would do when I arrived somewhere was pick up a bouquet of flowers and put them in my hotel room. It was amazing how just a bunch of flowers could transform a place. Even a hotel room.

So one day I bought some plants and put them on the window sill and another day I brought home some cut flowers and put them on the dining room table.

When I started bringing plants and flowers into the house the noises and nuisances stopped.

It was then I noticed how many vases there were around, and I discovered there were growing lights down in the basement. That suggested to me that someone liked gardening, that whoever it was, was a plant lover.

I know now it was Marion who loved the flowers and the garden.

I no longer feel threatened, although at first I did. The thing with the cabinet and the coughing at night, the sound of someone walking from room to room can get to you but I've learned to handle it.

I'm quite comfortable now.

I'm also curious as much as anything. Marion is a very strong presence and I believe she's here for a reason. I don't know if it's because all her things are still here and she feels unsettled or whether it's because of the way she died.

Her son told me his father had a girlfriend, maybe that has something to do with it.

Maybe her husband helped her along, out of her misery that is.

Who knows?

She's here, I know that. I suspect she may be here as long as the house is standing, or as long as it takes to do whatever it is she believes she has not completed. ðð

Ruby and Ernest: Haunted for more than Half a Century

When Ruby Smith heard that I was writing a book about ghosts she decided to call me one day, just to talk. She did not identify herself but said both she and her husband wanted, in fact needed, to share their experiences with someone.

Ruby and Ernest Smith are not their real names, but that does not make their bizarre experiences any less real. Both come from very small communities in which their families continue to live and they have no desire to put their children, or themselves, in a position where the telling of their stories might disrupt family life within the community.

The delicacy of their situation will become apparent as the stories unfold.

The first time Ruby called we talked for awhile and I assured her that I would respect their privacy. I was solidly hooked by the drama of their stories.

"I will talk to my husband about this," she told me during that first call, "and I promise you I will call back, even if we feel we are not able to tell our complete story."

A month passed and I had all but given up hope of hearing from her again but, true to her word, she did call. She and Ernest would visit me in my home and share their experiences with me and with my readers, she said.

The following stories span fifty years or more, beginning in the Second World War and continuing into the 1990s.

The first story is Ruby's alone. It is emotionally threatening and sets the scene for the ensuing stories of what this haunted couple, now senior citizens, have endured.

Regrettably space does not permit my including all their equally hair-raising and equally disturbing stories. They would make a book in themselves. ∂∂

A frightening forerunner

One of Ruby's stories begins at the time of her first marriage, during the Second World War. She and her first husband,William Harris, rented a small apartment in an old, three storey building in the north end of Saint John. She said it resembled a big old church or meeting house. The rooms were spacious and the staircase graceful and curving, complete with a carved bannister.

Although from the outside it looked "huge and spooky," inside it seemed pleasant enough. A Mr. and Mrs. Elliot from St. Martins had bought the house and they let it out in apartments, which Mrs. Elliot looked after while he worked at a logging camp in the St. Martins area.

The Harrises rented three rooms; a sitting room, a kitchen and a bedroom across the hall, just up from the bathroom which they shared with other tenants.

Here is Ruby's story. ঌঌ

This happened during the Second World War when my husband was in the army and stationed in Saint John. He was working in shifts and, from time-to-time, he would be told to work an extra shift. In those days telephones were hard to get and very few young couples had their own so William would call on Mrs. Elliot's telephone and ask to speak to me. On this particular night, he called to say that he would be working and would not be home until six o'clock the next morning.

I told Mrs. Elliot I thought I would go to bed early. I had my supper and tidied up then went to bed and fell asleep almost immediately. It must have been about one o'clock in the morning when I woke with a start from a deep sleep with shivers going up and down my spine. I had the feeling there was someone in my room and I sat bolt upright in bed, terrified!

I found myself staring straight into the eyes of a man who was standing at the foot of my bed and leering at me ... it's the only way to describe it.

I screamed at him! "What are you doing here? Get out of here! Get out!"

But he didn't move. He just stood there ...

"Mrs. Elliot! Mrs. Elliot!" I screamed, for it was her husband that was standing there. Or so I thought at the time.

I can still see him, after all these years. He was a big man. Over six feet tall and heavy and he was wearing a blue turtle neck sweater and dungarees with one strap over the shoulder.

Mrs. Elliot came and knocked at my door but I just kept screaming .

"Mrs. Harris," she said. "What is it? What is the matter? You've got to stop that noise! Mrs. Harris! My husband collapsed when we heard you screaming and I don't know what is the matter with him. He's terrified ...

"Mrs. Harris, why are you screaming? Please stop ... "

All I could seem to do was to keep on screaming because he was still standing there, you see. Leering at me. Then Mrs.Elliot turned the knob on the door and started to come in and, when she did that, the man turned around and walked across the room ... and right through the couch and then through the wall.

I was in shock.

"What *is* the matter?" Mrs. Elliot said when she came in the room.

I didn't know what to say. I was terrified but what could I say to her? She claimed her husband was having some kind of fit in their bedroom!

Finally I told her I must have had a nightmare or something and she was satisfied and left.

When my husband came home I told him what had happened and that I was too terrified to stay there alone again. We moved out of the house that week.

About three weeks later I met Mrs. Elliot uptown, at the head of King Street where Woolworth's was until recently. Back then it was Daniels' London House. It was the first time I had seen her since we moved out. I noticed immediately that the woman was wearing a black band on her arm, not an unusual situation in war time.

I remarked on it and asked who it was who died.

"My husband,"she said. "Not too long after you left."

She said that he and some of the men he worked with were coming home from the logging camp on a Friday night and, as often happened on a Friday payday, they had been drinking quite heavily.

"Three or four of them were in an old truck," she said.

They were roaming around town making a lot of noise and being a general nuisance. The police stopped them and said they would have to sleep it off in the jail house but that they could go home in the morning.

"The next morning when the police went into the cell they found my husband dead."

I don't know what you call it or how you explain it but I am sure that what I saw that night was Mr. Elliot's ghost. But I saw it before he died!

I can't explain it, I don't understand it but I do know that is what I saw. ◗◗

The life ... and death of Catherine

This story takes place in rural Kings County and it begins nearly fifty years ago when Ernest brought his war bride , Catherine, to Canada. He became a successful Kings County farmer and the home he shared with Catherine, and in which he raised his family, still stands. It is frequently vacant, he says, despite the low rent his son asks for it. Ernest describes the farm that he and Catherine bought as being "a pretty place surrounded by friendly people."

One of the oldest houses in the area, it was more than one hundred years old when they bought it in 1945. This is Ernest's story. ➤➤

I never did hear any stories about the house yet my wife complained of hearing strange noises there from the very beginning. I heard the same noises but I didn't let on to her. I told myself I didn't believe in haunted houses because I didn't want to say anything to scare her any more than she was.

We had a good farm and a good life. I would tell her all she was hearing was rats or squirrels scurrying through the walls. If it was spring I would say it was the frost coming out of the house that made the boards creak like footsteps. But I was uneasy all the same.

Eventually she stopped mentioning the noises, maybe she just got used to them ... I don't know.

If she saw anything that frightened her she didn't tell me about it.

We lived on the farm for forty years, then Catherine became ill. It was cancer. She was well into her seventies by then and eventually they had to take her into the hospital. She never wanted to leave that house. In her mind, she never did.

I would sit by her side in the hospital and talk to her and all the time she believed she was still in our farmhouse. She believed that right up to the day she died.

There was one particular day in the hospital I remember vividly. Catherine came out from under the heavy sedation she was on for the pain and, when she talked to me, she spoke quite rationally. I was pleased and thought her mind was clearing ... until she looked right at me and said, "Ernest there's a piece of rope there on the floor. Pick it up before someone trips over it!"

Another time she asked me if the cat had come home yet.

"It's snowing very hard out there and it's cold," she said.

She was talking about a big, black tomcat we had that used to take off in every kind of weather. Blizzards or violent rain storms were all the same to him.

But that day was a beautiful, warm day in spring. In Catherine's mind it was a winter day and she was at home. She never left the house, you see?

When she was alive she had no desire to ever leave. One time a neighbour came over and suggested that we should take a little trip somewhere. He said they would look after the cattle while we were gone.

Catherine wouldn't hear of it. "No," she said, "I have no desire to go anywhere. Everything I want is right here. Pure clean fresh air, my children, my farm. Wild horses will never haul me out." That's how strongly she felt.

I stayed on at the farm after she died and gradually began my new life without her.

It was about three months after she died that I woke up with a start at about two o'clock in the morning. I was sitting straight up in bed and looking out the window.

The moon was full and bright, shining through the trees in the orchard and right into the bedroom. It was a beautiful sight. I sat there, looking out at the night for awhile then turned around to lie back down again with my back to the light ... and I couldn't believe my eyes!

There, in the bed beside me in the exact place and in the way she always slept, her arms outside the covers, was Catherine. It was as if she had never got ill and gone to the hospital.

I knew my wife was dead, yet here she was beside me. I couldn't understand what was happening. I thought

I must have been dreaming so I fought back the fear and forced myself to reach out and touch her arm.

It was hard. Stone-cold hard flesh.

Right then and there I must have keeled over for I don't remember another thing until I awoke the next morning. Then it all came back to me in a flash, vividly.

I scrambled out of that bed as fast as I could and I grabbed the covers and my clothes and I went downstairs and made up my bed on the couch down there. I never slept in that bedroom again until after Ruby and I were married.

A few weeks later I went to the doctor for my regular checkup. He sent me to have an ECG, which surprised me. The doctor always told me I had the heart and the lungs of a young man..

"Your heart is badly scarred," he said when the reports came back. And he asked me if I had suffered any chest pains recently.

I didn't tell him what I suspected. That I must have had a heart attack at the time that my dead wife appeared in my bed.

Ernest and Ruby move to the farm

When Ernest and Ruby were first married they lived in her home near Saint John until she arranged her affairs there. Later they moved to Ernest's farm. Ruby's 14 year-old grand-daughter, Lila, who had been living with her for a number of years, moved with them.

Around the same time another of Ruby's daughters took ill with the flu and they suggested she and her small child should come to the country where Ruby could care for her.

Every day Lila helped look after Emily, carrying trays upstairs and keeping her company.

Ruby and Ernest had given Emily and her child the master bedroom and they were sleeping downstairs on the couch.

Unknown to Ruby and Ernest, Lila was being wakened every night by someone opening her bedroom door. She thought it was either Ruby or Ernest teasing her because no one ever answered when she asked 'Who's there?' but she could sense someone's presence.

So Lila plotted to 'trap' whoever it was. The ceiling light had a long cord and one night Lila moved her bed over close enough that she could lie in bed while holding the end of the cord. She pulled the cord to turn off the light then waited.

Promptly on time her door clicked open. The minute she heard the door she pulled the cord and shouted 'Aaaagh ...' But there was no one there.

She jumped out of bed and ran downstairs to where Ernest and Ruby were in the living room.

"So it wasn't you!" She said, looking at them where Ruby was comfortably curled up beside Ernest on the couch.

They asked her what she meant and she explained what she thought was a 'trick' meant to tease her.

Ernest told her that she was living in an old house and that often the doors in old houses don't latch well. He said that probably there was something at that time of night, someone going upstairs, or walking in the hallway, that made the floor shift and the door open.

Lila went back up to bed, only half-convinced that what Ernest said was true and, without telling either Ruby or Ernest she took the outside latch off her door and put it on the inside.

The next night she also barricaded the door with a chair under the handle and followed the same procedure as the night before, holding the light cord in her hand but lying in bed with the door wedged closed and securely latched.

Right on time the door flew open, the chair careered across the room and Lila pulled the light switch only to face an empty doorway.

"She said the hair on her neck stood up on end and she froze in her bed, terrified and screaming. When Ernest and I came upstairs she jumped out of bed, raced past us and down the stairs, sobbing. The poor girl said she would never sleep in that room again so we made up a cot for her in another room downstairs."

One night Lila had been in Emily's room reading when she decided to get up and go downstairs for a snack. Just as she was about to start down the stairs a woman suddenly appeared, standing there with one foot on a step and looking up the stairs.

"Gram!" she shrieked, "What are you trying to do ... scare me?"

She immediately realized it was a woman she had never seen before coming up the stairs.

She said, "Oh, sorry. You're not Gram.," and turned around and went into Emily's room to tell her about thinking she saw Ruby on the stairs. When she came back out the woman was gone.

"Lila came down and asked us who the woman was that she had seen on the stairs. We told her there was no one else here," Ruby said.

"But I saw her," Lila insisted. "She was a stocky woman with grey hair that came straight to her ears and she was wearing a cardigan sweater and lace-up shoes."

Lila told Ruby that she stared at the woman, who was then only a short distance away from her, and she said the woman stared back at her but didn't say anything.

"After Lila went back upstairs to her room Ernest turned to me and his face was as white as that of any ghost. 'That was Catherine she described!' he said.

"Lila had given us a perfect description of Ernest's first wife although she had never seen the woman in her life. She had never heard her described and, to our best knowledge, had never so much as seen a picture of the woman."

By this time Ernest and Ruby were beginning to feel a bit shook up about the things that were going on and Ernest finally told Ruby, for the first time, about finding Catherine in his bed. Neither of them could understand what was happening but, although they were puzzled over it, they didn't feel threatened in any way at that time.

As Ernest told Ruby, Catherine loved her home and just didn't want to leave it. They decided it was probably her opening Lila's door, just like any mother checking on her children at night before going to bed herself.

Ruby had long before concluded that another world exists around us, although we are not always tuned in to it.

"That's not to say that I understand anything of what has happened to me, to Ernest or to any of us, particularly while we were living in our farm home. In the beginning I had no sense of fear, nor did Ernest. I could understand Catherine's feelings and I do believe her spirit exists there in a life separate from ours.

"It was not Catherine who forced us to leave our home. It was something else entirely."

One afternoon, after the girls had left to return to Saint John, Ruby and Ernest were waltzing around the living room to some music on the radio. While they were dancing they heard a door slam and then the sound of heavy footsteps walking across the kitchen floor, past the room where they were dancing and then continue on up the stairs.

Ruby said, "Who was that?"

Ernest said he thought it was probably his son. Ruby wondered why he didn't come in and Ernest said he would go upstairs and see what he wanted.

When he went upstairs there was no one up there.

"We felt uneasy about it, and rightly so it seems now because that was just the beginning of the real trouble that would come our way before we finally gave up and left."

Things like furniture, ornaments and other small items started being moved around in their house.

"Early on, when Catherine had complained about the noises and what she felt were 'hauntings' in the house I brushed them off, giving her excuses for the things she heard. But those same sounds remained unexplained to me and they bothered me at the time, although I never acknowledged it. Not even to myself, really. I was busy with my outside work much of the time but Catherine's life was spent in the house, living closely with whatever was going on.

"Now, in retrospect, I believe that whatever it was, it was and is evil."

On a regular basis Ruby and Ernest began to hear what sounded like something being dragged across the floor upstairs. Ernest would then go upstairs and look around in every room.

"There's no one up there," he would tell Ruby and there was nothing out of place.

Ernest was getting something out of the deep freeze one day when the hair on the back of his neck began to stand straight up, for no reason other than the feeling that there was someone or something behind him.

"The freezer is near the stairs, the same stairs where Ruby's grand-daughter had seen Catherine. I was afraid of what I might see if I turned around. I was afraid that Catherine was standing behind me and I truly did not know what would happen to me if, indeed, it was her. Perhaps I would have another heart attack, only this time I feared if I did I would be joining Catherine in that other world.

"But even while all of this was going through my mind I was turning to look behind me, toward the stairs.

"But it wasn't Catherine on the stairs, it was a strange man in old-fashioned working clothes. I blinked my eyes in surprise and he was gone. As fast as that."

The noises and the strange activities became more and more frequent. One day Ernest returned from an errand to find Ruby outside the house, shivering in fear and cold. She had been standing in the kitchen when the noise of something being moved in almost every room upstairs started again. Then she could hear what sounded like something being dragged across the floor with a lot of clanging and banging.

"I was terrified," Ruby said. "I was frozen not just by the noise and commotion but by the feeling that I was being watched. My eyes were drawn over toward the door and, as I looked, the door handle started turning. I thought someone was coming in. I hoped it was Ernest.

But nothing happened. No one came in and the door handle stopped turning. "I decided that I should either go out that door myself or go out through the window if I had to. I just knew I had to get out of the house.

"The doors at the farm never stick, they always open easily and smoothly. But that day when I tried to open the kitchen door I couldn't. I pulled and I tugged but nothing happened. I could feel myself getting hysterical and I really was ready to jump through the window, never mind the danger of the broken glass. Then, suddenly, whatever was holding the door let go and I went crashing back against the wall.

"I ran from the kitchen and into the porch but when I tried to open that door the same thing happened. I pulled and tugged and by this time I was crying and sobbing ... again the door suddenly opened, flinging me against the wall."

She was still sobbing hysterically when Ernest found her. Again he went in the house and up the stairs and looked through all the rooms.

There was no one anywhere. There was no sign of anyone having been outside or having driven up in a car.

As Ernest was about to go downstairs to reassure Ruby that all was well, a knocking started in the walls.

"It was as if they were telling me 'Yes we are here.'

"Then from downstairs I heard a door slam and Ruby screaming. When I got there she told me she felt something brush past her and the the door was suddenly flung open and then shut again with a bang."

"It was as if someone or something had passed by me and gone out of the house," Ruby said.

More things started disappearing, often silly things like a shoe would disappear and be nowhere to be found, then it would suddenly appear in some ludicrous place.

Night after night they could hear a steady pounding of feet going up and down stairs ... but not the house stairs ... stairs that used to go up from the living room, where Ruby and Ernest were now sleeping. Stairs that weren't there any more because Ernest had torn them out and built the new ones when he bought the house in 1945.

Ernest believes that the ghosts or spirits from a time long before he ever bought the house were now going up and down those old stairs. Often the footsteps sounded like children running up and down and he now believes those sounds were always there and account for some of the sounds Catherine complained of hearing. He also believes that when her spirit joined the others in the house it set off a frantic chain of activity that had not, to his knowledge, existed before.

"Ruby and I have identified four different entities, not counting the children, that we believe exist there. My wife Catherine and three others. The three others are from another time and they include the workman I saw when I was at the freezer and two others that are upstairs all the time. We believe they may be reenacting something that happened in the house a very long time ago."

"I know now that one of them was a woman," Ruby said. "After we moved out Ernest wanted to go back and get something he had forgotten. We drove out there and I waited in the car out front. Something, a movement ... I don't know what ... drew my attention to the second floor window that faced up the driveway. There was a woman standing there. It wasn't Catherine, it was someone from an earlier time. Whoever it was, was wearing a dress with long tight sleeves that were puffy at the top."

One winter day Ruby and Ernest went back to the house once more to get some things they wanted for their new home. They took Ruby's daughter Emily and her little girl, who was about four years old by then, with them. Ruby was watching Emily and Ernest take down a chandelier in the dining room when her grand-daughter called from upstairs.

"Grampy!" she said. "There's a car coming up the driveway."

"We could all hear the car by then," Ruby said, "so I went to the door to see who it was. There was no car. There were no tracks of any car, except for ours.

"We never went back again."

Ernest sold the farm to his son, keeping some acreage on the water for a summer cottage for he and Ruby. His son refuses to believe that the house is haunted, but he has never lived there since he was a boy. He rents the house out from time to time but tenants don't last too long and tend to leave in a hurry and without reason.

Ruby believes they are scared off, although neither she nor Ernest has ever talked to them.

The mystery of what happened on the farm, perhaps one hundred years ago or more, that causes the restless spirits to keep reenacting the event will probably never be known.

As for Catherine's ghost Ernest is quite comfortable with that.

"You couldn't meet a sweeter soul than Catherine. She was one of the kindest, finest women who ever lived," he says. "If her spirit needs to stay on in the house, then so be it. I don't believe hers is a restless spirit or anything like that. I think Catherine is just where she is, and was, the happiest.

"As for the rest of the stuff going on there I just don't know. We'll never know, not in this life anyway." औौ

The protective nun who wasn't there

Kate, like her mother and her great-grandmother before her, was born with a veil over her face. This is said to be a sign that she would be one of the gifted who can see beyond this mortal coil. Kate will not spend the night of January 7 in her parents' Hampton home. January 7 is the date of the one time that she remembers having seen what is commonly called 'a ghost'. In her mother's memory it is the second such experience that she knows Kate to have had. Kate is reluctant to tell her stories, they are related here by her mother.

The nuns were excited when Kate was born. They were superstitious about the veil over her face and insisted we should keep it. My mother, a puritanical protestant, wouldn't hear of it and told the nuns to throw it away but my Roman Catholic grandmother insisted on taking it home with her. She kept it in a covered jar at her house for years. I don't know now whatever happened to it.

Interesting, though. Isn't it? To be born with a veil over one's face has been the subject of folklore for centuries. I remember the nuns and my grandmother saying that it was good luck, that a dog would never bite Kate and no house she was living in would ever burn.

That sends chills down my spine just thinking of it because I still vividly remember when the house next door to us burned down when we were living in Campbellton. The houses were so close together they were almost touching, probably no more than a foot between them. It was a terrible fire and everyone thought it was a miracle that our house didn't catch fire too ...do you know the outside wall wasn't even scorched!

I've been known to scoff a bit at the supernatural but Kate's experiences have convinced me that there must be something to metaphysical happenings. What, I don't pretend to know.

Kate was just a toddler when we were living in the Northwest Territories and the first of her experiences with the supernatural took place.

I'll never forget it. Kate herself doesn't remember it of course, she was too young. I was making fruitcake in the kitchen and my oldest son was crawling around the floor. He had just made his way to the hall when the doorbell rang. I told Kate to go see who was at the door which meant she had to go through the hall.

She was only about three years old at the time but she knew immediately that something was wrong with her brother and she came running back to me and said, 'Mummy, come quick, the baby's choking!'

I raced out to the hall and sure enough, he was. I grabbed him and managed to dislodge a chunk of cellophane mixed with sticky fruit from his throat. Later I asked Kate if she had answered the door. She said 'yes' that it was a nun but she wasn't there any more.

I looked out the door but there was no one in sight, nor was there any sign of footprints in the snow or any indication of a vehicle having driven by in the past hour or more. I found that really strange since it was winter and the snow was blowing at its usual rate around the house.

I asked Kate to describe her to me and, when she did, I knew exactly who it was. I had seen pictures of this nun, she was called Sister Rosalie. One of the men in the area had been doing research on her and had made contact with a woman who lived 500 miles away and who claimed to be the nun's medium! Sister Rosalie was known to be a benefactor of the people of the north. I believe she came to our door in order to save my son from choking to death.

Kate met Kate's ghost on January 7

The very first night we spent in our home when we moved back to New Brunswick, I knew the house was haunted. Haunted, moreover, by a noisy ghost who dwells in between the walls of our bedroom and that of our oldest son. But it is Kate who has actually seen the ghost and, because Kate saw her, we have actually been able to identify the woman visitor. We believe she is visible every January

7, probably the day she died because it is two days before her funeral.

She is another Kate. The ghost of Kate Colwell dwells in our house, she has even tended the wood fire on occasion when I have been called away.

The two Kates met when my Kate started downstairs about two o'clock in the morning because she thought she heard one of her brothers down there and wanted to know what was going on.

She only got as far as the turn in the stairs when she was stopped in her tracks. At the foot of the stairs, but in a setting quite different from the way it is now, sat a lady dressed all in black rocking back and forth, back and forth in a rocking chair that does not exist in our house!

Kate bolted back up the stairs and into bed where she pulled the covers over her head and shivered for the rest of the night. She was too terrified even to come across the hall and wake her father and me.

The next day she gave us a very vivid description of the woman, how she was dressed and what the entrance hall looked like.

Curious, I contacted the people who had owned the house before us and eventually we were able to get a bunch of photographs of the people who lived here at the turn of the century. We sorted through them and there she was! Just as Kate described her. Stern and cranky looking Kate Colwell. We went on from there and did a bit more research and discovered that her funeral had taken place on January 9, 1902, two days after the date Kate saw her.

Ever since then Kate has refused to stay in the house on that date. We have all tried to see her but although we can sense her presence from time to time we have yet to experience what Kate did. ﻬﻬ

Mrs. Langstroth and Hampton's Wayside Inn

When we first moved to Hampton in 1962 there was a marvellous old house, near the Courthouse, called the Wayside Inn. Three storeys high and half a city block long, it was the home of the Langstroth family, Bill Langstroth's grandparents actually. (Bill, one of Hampton's famous sons, produced the Don Messer Show in the early days of television then produced and emceed Singalong Jubilee where Anne Murray blossomed to fame and later became Mrs. Bill Langstroth.)

In the 1960s the Wayside Inn was owned by the late Harley Dunham who loved to tell the story of how they always knew when a thunder and lightening storm was about to erupt. He said old Mrs. Langstroth would be seen clutching her purse to her bosom and pacing, back and forth, along the third floor hall.

I called Bill to ask him what he knew about his grandmother's ghost and here's what he had to say. ཉ༙

It sounds like something she would do. I bet she'd hang right in there.

To be honest with you I don't ever remember hearing that story about her, but it doesn't surprise me in the least, particularly the clutching the purse part.

Her name was Helena Gertrude Smith before she married my grandfather, William Langstroth, and she was quite a woman in her time.

My grandfather built the Wayside Inn for a family named Dickson who made a bust of it, so my grandmother bought it and ran it up to almost the time of the Second World War. She operated it like a rest home for a time. She would take in the sick or elderly and look after them.

She was a very high-principled Victorian lady and, as kids, we found her very unapproachable. We never thought of her as having a sense of humour until after she died and we found a book of jokes she had written in a scribbler. It seems that when the drummers (travelling salesmen) came to stay she would serve them coffee then go into another room where she could listen and copy down the jokes they told each other over their coffee.

But do I think she haunts the place? I wouldn't be surprised at all but that she would hang right in there as long as the building remains standing. ➷

The priestly time traveller

Bob Wishart is a part-time teacher in Hampton and has followed a number of careers in his life including some time as a newspaper reporter and photographer. He firmly believes that, from time to time, spirits of people from the past can be felt and seen. For lack of a better description he thinks of them as 'time travellers'. ぷ

It was November 1988, a dirty, rotten, cold Saturday morning, around eight o'clock or so, when I saw this canoeist paddling along through the marsh. He was quite a distance away but I had my camera with me and I had a bit of a zoom lens on it so I scuttled down the bank there and I took his picture. I called out to him a few times before he disappeared around the bend but he never let on if he heard me.

I thought it might be someone I knew and I wondered what they were doing out in that marsh in a canoe at the end of November. I processed the film and blew it up large and what to my wondering eyes should appear but a figure right out of my grade eight history book!

When I was a kid in grade eight we used to study something called *The Jesuits Among the Hurons* and this figure, in what to all intents and purposes turned out to be a birch bark canoe, was none other than a Jesuit priest! He was wearing a black cassock, a clerical collar and a broad-brimmed tricorn hat ... not a George Wash-

Illustration done from Bob Wishart photograh

ington type of tricorn but the kind a priest might be wearing.

   Since I did the film processing myself I thought I would take it to some professionals and see what they could do with it to make it clearer. They were able to get a little better image but it is still grainy, although you can see plainly what it is.

   That marsh area was once a main thoroughfare, it was how the Indians and the settlers got around from place to place and I really believe that what I saw was what you might call a time traveller. I think he came through the curtain for a few minutes from some time back in the 1600s.

That couldn't be her
... she died over three years ago!

Bob shared another experience with someone else.

It was around Hallowe'en, wouldn't you know! We were driving along the road in the Bloomfield area when we saw this woman all dressed in white. She was wearing a large fisherman-knit type white sweater and white dress and she was walking along off to the side of the road.

I didn't think anything of it at the time but when we got to my friend's place, two or three farms up the road, he looked at me kind of strange-like and said, "You know who that was, don't you?"

I said, "No. Who was it?"

"It was Mrs. Waller," he said. "But it couldn't be her, she died three or four years ago."

We went back to where we were when we saw her and looked over to where she had been walking. It was a ditch. A deep ditch and it was filled with dirty water.

"That's where the old road used to go," my friend said.

It was eerie. Really eerie. This white spectre had been just gliding along on the top of the ditch. It was the spectre of an old woman, which she was when she died, not a young one which she would have been when the road was there.

I don't know whether she had been laid out in that white outfit when she died or why she was wearing it. I also don't know if it being close to Hallowe'en had anything to do with it or not. I just know what we both saw. Plain as day. ৯৯

Doreen Damon will never drown, she still has her veil

Doreen Damon is one of that fascinating group of those with second sight whose birth was marked by the presence of a cowl, or veil as Doreen's mother called it, covering their heads.

"There was a real superstition about the veil," she said. "I was born at home and when my grandmother went to wipe my eyes she couldn't get to them because they were covered over with this veil. She told me that the midwife just touched the bottom of it and it slipped right off."

Doreen still has that veil, and for good reason. "I was told that sailors would pay a fortune for it but my mother said, 'give up every cent you have but don't ever give up your veil. You will never drown as long as you keep it.' That's why the sailors want it ... You see?"

An English war-bride, Doreen and husband Hazen Damon have made their home in New Brunswick. They owned and managed a number of Save Easy supermarkets, most recently in Hampton where they have now retired and their children are carrying on the business.

Here, then, are two stories from Doreen's life . ঌঌ

The Dream Message

We were living in Lakewood Heights, in Saint John at the time this happened. In Canada people will pull the drapes or the blinds of a house if someone dies but it is far different from the part of England where I lived. The custom there is for the entire street, or block, to draw their shades or curtains when someone on that street dies.

One night I dreamed that I went home on a whim and, when I drove down the street in the taxi, all the houses had their curtains drawn and I wondered who had died. When I got to my mother's house and went to the door it opened and someone said, *You're too late, Doreen, she's dead.*

I said, 'No, she's not!' I went over to her in the coffin and I picked her up and hugged her and she opened her eyes.

Not too long after that dream my family contacted me to say they got together and decided they had to tell me about Mum. They said she had cancer and wasn't expected to live much longer. My mother had never been one to complain about illness and I didn't get to see her very often so I didn't know her health was failing.

I immediately got on a plane and went to England and was able to spend some time with her. A short time after I got home they called to tell me she had died, content that I had been there for her.

I was napping on the couch one day, not too long after my mother's death, when something woke me up very suddenly. It was the feel of a little hand on mine.

I opened my eyes and looked up and there was my mother, going up the stairs of the house we were living in.

It broke me up all over again. ᴘᴘ

Don't You Dig in My Garden!

We opened a store in Chipman in the mid-1970s and had a terrible time trying to find a place to live. Many a night we slept on top of the freezers until we heard about a house that was available at Briggs Corner. A young couple rented it to us. Her mother, who owned the house, had just died there and they were working in Toronto.

It was a bit of a dreary house and our son Allen didn't like it at all. He was old enough to stay at home alone but he wouldn't stay in the house by himself, even in the day time. He would come to the store with us instead.

It was winter when we moved in and when the snow was finally gone I thought it would be a good time to put some bulbs in beside the cement walk. Hazen had gone to the store, the children were at school and I was at home by myself.

I went outside carrying my trusty trowel and a bunch of bulbs, intending to plant them. But as soon as I crouched down and put my trowel in the earth there was a sharp rapping on the front window. It sounded as if someone's knuckles were just a-goin' hard against that window pane.

I looked up, startled, wondering who was in my house, but I knew there was no one there. I also knew right away that those knuckles were telling me to stop digging. So I stopped digging!

Sure enough, come spring that place where I had been digging was just filled with flowers.

It seems the lady didn't want her garden disturbed. ≈

Are children's imaginary friends ...really ghosts?

Doris Calder, Kingston Peninsula native, educator, historian and world traveller has always felt sensitive to the presence of ghosts or spirits but has never experienced them in her own home. There are, however, numerous ghosts on the Peninsula, she says, and she has experienced the presence of at least one of these. As well, she has met the famous ghost at the home of the late Pat Jenkins of the Loomcrofters in Gagetown and another while visiting an aunt in the United States. Here are her thoughts on these phenomena and her experiences of them.

There is what was once a boarding house at Clifton Royal that both a pharmacist and a shipbuilder are said to haunt. Some girls who used to babysit there said they experienced a presence in the house all the time.

I went to the house one time with some relatives from the States, whose grandmother used to live there, and as soon as I started walking through the house I knew there was a presence in the dining room. It is always colder in the place where the ghost is and that day I felt the ghost go right by me.

The feeling of cold that comes from the presence of a ghost is a different kind of cold than ordinary cold rooms. It's hard to explain except to say it's a dead cold.

The ghosts in this Clifton house used to rattle the dishes and move things around and the people who lived there could never keep the attic door shut, that's where the shipbuilder used to sleep.

The couple who owned the house said their grown son would pile things in front of the door to try and keep it closed but invariably it would open.

About ten years ago I went to Connecticut to visit my cousin Bill who lives in a very old house near Danburry, that dates from 1635. It used to be a rural farm area.

I had heard that there was a presence there, that of an elderly woman who used to sit in an armchair. Children see her frequently. They pass her on the stairs and say 'Hi!, How are you?' Of course she never answers but apparently she gets annoyed when they turn the television off because she turns it right back on again.

My cousin came home from grocery shopping one day when there was no one home. Juggling two arms full of parcels while fishing around in her purse for keys she was surprised when the door was opened for her. Just like that! There was no one there and the door had been locked!

I believe there are natural presences and supernatural presences. That, like water in a sponge, we're intermingled but we just can't see each other. Children may see them (ghosts) better because they haven't been taught not to.

This, I believe, accounts for those imaginary friends children have. They're really what we call ghosts. ঌঌ

In Cambridge a benevolent presence, a prankster and a live spirit co-exist

Bobbie Hallum's 19th Century farmhouse stands primly and properly on the bank of the Washademoak Lake in Queens County. Its architecture is in the stern, gabled storey-and-a-half style of the time.

Over the years an extension was added providing a roomy new kitchen, pantry and storage area on the ground floor and a fifth bedroom and storage space upstairs, where creative nooks and crannies reflect the whims of the steeply pitched roof and gable windows.

Off the original kitchen, now Bobbie's living room, there is a birthing nook, a cosy alcove that could be curtained off for privacy while remaining close to the warmth of the chimney. Across the entrance hall is the original parlour, now Bobbie's bedroom.

This pattern of rooms on the ground level allows her to function efficiently from her wheelchair, to which she has been confined since a car accident left her without the use of her legs.

She bought the 150-year-old MacDonald house because its silent voices welcomed her. They assured her that here was the peace and seclusion she needed after years in a high-stress government job.

"If there is some sort of presence here it is certainly a pleasant one, even the dogs recognize it as non-threatening. At times they will be looking at empty space, their expressions more of curiosity than anything else. Yet if anyone or anything comes near the door it's 'Rrrfff Rrrfff Rrrrfff' the whole time."

The following four stories relate to Bobby Hallum and the presences that share her home. ৯৯

A lesson in history

Just after I bought this house my brother, who lives in British Columbia, came here to visit me. He maintains that I didn't just 'find' this place by accident. He claims he senses a very strong presence in the house and he believes I was guided here for some reason. He also believes that it is a woman's presence and that it is very akin to me.

I think there is something to what he says. I have always felt comfortable here, and protected.

It is strange how I found the place. I happened to be browsing through the newspaper one day, reading through the real estate ads out of curiosity as much as anything, when I saw the ad for this house. I said to my daughter, 'you know that's pretty country down there, I think I'll check this place out.'

I saw the driveway first of all and thought to myself, *this is a mistake!* It's a long, narrow driveway off a sparsely populated road.

Then I saw the house.

Omigod! I thought. *If I can get around in this place then I want it! This is the place for me.*

A man I was seeing at the time told me I would never be able to live here. He was against it, but that's okay because we broke up anyway.

From the beginning my sister and I agreed with my brother that the presence in the house was female and we named her Martha. The second presence, the poltergeist prankster, I suspect is a child, probably a boy.

Quite by accident I discovered who I believe the female presence actually is.

When I moved in here I had this strange dream every night. It was nothing spectacular, in fact if anything it was very simple but it just kept repeating itself every night and for the life of me I couldn't figure out what it was all about.

To begin with, I have never been in the basement of the house. I do look down the stairs every time I open the door because I feed my cats at the head of the basement stairs. My dream involved that basement. I dreamt that I went into the basement through the outside basement door and that when I was in I turned to the right and there was a big hole in the basement wall with rocks piled up to close it off. In my dream I took down the rocks and I found all these Indian artifacts piled up in there.

That's all there was to the dream. Nothing ever happened. Just the same dream every night. A big hole in the wall with rocks piled up, a sort of cave and Indian artifacts.

After I had been here for awhile I told one of my neighbours about the dream and I asked him if he knew anything about Indians being around the area.

He looked at me strangely and he said yes, in the old days, there were lots of Indians around, but didn't I know the story about the woman who owned my house during the early nineteenth century?

I confessed my ignorance.

He told me that one time two men in the area were said to have got into a duel for some reason, although duelling had been outlawed by that time. Anyway, during the duel one man killed the other and the authorities were out to arrest him. This woman, whose name I have since learned was *Janet,* hid him in the basement.

Now I have to admit that a part of the story they told me doesn't make much sense to me, but they claim that the man dug a tunnel from the basement of the house to the lake so he could escape on a boat. There were militia stationed near here at the time and they patrolled the lake constantly, watching for people trying to leave by the lake and get down the St. John River to the city where they could disappear safely.

What that duel has to do with my dream I don't

know, except that it does seem to connect with an opening down in what was then, I suppose, an earth cellar with rock walls.

The rock walls are still there, but at some time a cement foundation was put in and cement poured around the rock walls to reinforce them.

The odd thing is that there is an indentation on the front lawn that goes all the way to the lake.

Of course the other thing it does is give some indication of what sort of person this Janet was. Again, during the course of the events that follow, I discovered that her diaries play a large part in *Those Days Are Gone Away*, a history of Queens County written by Marion Gilchrist Reicker.

Janet (Hendry) MacDonald was born in this house and she lived here all her life. Her diary was written on scraps of paper, the backs of calendar sheets, anything she could find to write on. It is a wonderful insight into life here in the first half of the nineteenth century. Unfortunately it doesn't begin until she is forty, but even then it is quite wonderful.

She was born Feb. 7, 1795, the eldest daughter of George Hendry and Susan Bulyea, and she died in 1887 at the ripe old age of 92. As far as I can tell she lived most of those years in this house. Her diary covers the years from 1857 to 1868. Janet and her husband, Alexander MacDonald, raised six sons and one daughter all of whom, save one who died young, lived to ripe old ages as well. One son, William, a dentist in Boston, lived 101 years!

I firmly believe that it is Janet who is the presence I feel in this house. I believe that, for some unknown reason she has never left it.

The Poltergeist Prankster

While I do feel there is a presence in this house that does not threaten me in any way, I also experience what I think of as a poltergeist kind of activity. It's as if there is a devilish child, a prankster, teasing me. For example; I am forever and constantly missing things ... like the big plastic jug I poured juice out of less than a week ago. It's totally gone. Vamoosed! And there's been no one else staying here at the house except me for weeks!

The strange thing is that maybe next week, next month or next year it will turn up again, sitting out somewhere in plain sight!

But that's not the strangest thing this teasing presence does. My clocks are constantly totally out of sync. They're erratic. The hands won't stay in place. Recently, my son was here from Halifax and helped me put new batteries in this one (*a kitchen wall clock out of Bobbie's reach*) and we carefully set it so the hands were dead on. Now, the minute hand is totally off! Okay, so that's mechanical and maybe it can be explained mechanically, but hear this!

My sister went off to Aruba about two years ago and she left her Grandmother Clock with me for safekeeping. So I said to my daughter, 'I'm not going to wind that clock because as sure as I do I'll overwind it, or underwind it, or do something foolish and that will be the end of it.'

It hung on the wall for eight months until one day, when the young man that does my lawns was here, I heard this strange noise.

'What's that noise?' I asked him.

He looked at me as if I was nuts and said, 'It sounds like a clock bonging to me.'

'I don't have a clock that bongs,' I told him.

So we came in the house, counting the bongs as we went. There were twelve of them in all. It was noon hour and there was my sister's clock, after eight months of silence, bonging away with the hands set dead on twelve o'clock.

Eight months and there hadn't been a peep out of that clock. Then it started up and it went for eight days, bonging away on the hours, half-and-quarter-hours. Then it stopped again and I haven't heard a sound out of it since.

I don't have any feeling of this particular presence when it's around, I just see and hear what it's up to and, once or twice, I have experienced something directly.

There was one time when I was going through the house turning all the lights off before I went to bed and as I came down the hall by the stairs my chair suddenly stopped dead. No matter what I did it just wouldn't move. I was stuck there.

I tried and tried, but that chair would not budge.

So I sat there, trying to decide what I was going to do until suddenly I felt the chair release. It was as if someone had been leaning over the stairs and holding the push handles and just held me there for awhile then let go. It was like some sort of practical joke.

Then, one day, I was in the kitchen and going toward the back door when suddenly the top bolt-latch came down and the key went flying out of the lock and onto the floor. Obviously someone didn't want me going out.

I just laughed and said, 'All right Martha' ... that's what we call her even though we are pretty sure now that the presence is Janet ... anyway I said, 'all right, I wasn't planning to go out right now anyway.'

Later I got my tongs and my stick, picked up the key and unlocked the bolt.

Of course now I realize that it probably wasn't Janet/Martha at all but this other prankish presence that I still haven't identified.

Possessive presence threatens house guests

There is one room upstairs where almost everyone who sleeps there, or tries to sleep there, complains that they can hear voices all night. They say it is more like murmurings, because they can't make out what the voices are saying but they definitely identify the murmuring sounds as coming from voices.

I call that my son's room because it is where he sleeps when he comes to visit. He is big, rugged and down to earth. I would say he is the last person in our family who would ever have anything to do with something that might be even remotely considered spiritual or other-worldly.

He has never complained about any of the things that the others talk about but one night he did have a rather strange experience that he found a bit frightening at the time it happened, but in no way threatening.

He came down to breakfast one morning and said 'Mom, you know how I always sleep with my feet outside the covers? Well, last night I was dozing off to sleep when something stroked my foot, ever so gently. I didn't dare open my eyes to see what it was, I just pulled my feet up under the blankets!'

I told him it was probably an animal of some sort, although my cats always sleep in the basement and the dogs sleep beside my bed. He just shook his head and said, 'Mom, that was no animal!'

My nephew's girlfriend woke up the whole house one night with the most blood-curdling scream you could ever imagine. My sister went flying up the stairs to check it out and here was this girl standing in the hall, bug-eyed.

She told my sister, 'I can't sleep in that room! Some girl came in and woke me up and said, *I don't want*

I don't want you here!

you here! She was threatening to hit me.'

We quieted her down and let her sleep in the birthing nook in the living-room for the rest of the night. We didn't tell her that other people have felt uneasy sleeping in there, too.

I find that the people who have the worst time sleeping upstairs are usually people who have other upsets and difficulties in their lives. Some of my relatives insist on sleeping with the light on while other relatives claim they get the best night's sleep you could imagine and can't understand what all the fuss is about.

I used to have a baby bed here that belonged to the MacDonald's, the original owners of the house. It was hand-made of wood with a horsehair mattress and

it was in the room opposite the one I get all the complaints about. For some reason a lot of people were uneasy about that baby bed and no one ever wanted to
sleep in the same room with it. They said it made them
feel cold.

I have no idea what was behind that but I finally
gave the bed away, yet that room still has a cold feeling
they tell me, even without the bed being there. Perhaps
it has something to do with the person who tried, and
succeeded, in chasing my nephew's girlfriend away.
Maybe someone is protecting a baby that died there. Who
knows?

Bobbie's spirit haunts her house

Perhaps the strangest experience we have had involves my daughter and I being here, in this house, when we were both away.

I went to Halifax about a year ago to visit my son and I took my dog with me. My daughter was in Fredericton that weekend.

When I got back one of my neighbours came over and said, 'I want to thank your daughter for letting Huntley in to use the telephone the day he nearly drowned.'

I said, 'Oh, that's no problem.'

When my daughter came home I said, ' You didn't tell me Huntley nearly drowned!'

She said, 'I didn't know Huntley nearly drowned.'

I said, 'Well, you let him in to make a phone call.'

She said, 'Mom. I haven't been home since you left!'

Another neighbour across the field said, 'Who was staying at the house while you were away?'

I said, 'Nobody.'

'Well there was a woman your age waving to me from the window, she even looked like you.'

Two people claimed there was someone here in the house and both of them thought it was either me or my daughter. They are people who know both of us. There wasn't so much as a tea bag missing or a cup out of place ... nothing. The house was still locked up tight, just the way I left it.

Later I saw Huntley and his wife and I said to him, 'Huntley, it wasn't Bobbie who let you in to use the telephone that day. Can you describe the person for me?'

He looked at me rather oddly and he looked at his wife and then he said, 'Well, you were there.'

Now I'm in a wheelchair, I'm rather hard to mistake for someone else and I wasn't here that weekend. Neither was my daughter.

I called everyone I could think of that might feel free to come in here if I was away. Not a soul said they were even near the place. ɷɷ

There are ghosts ...
and then there are ghosts?

Among those in the first category is innkeeper Jim Leslie. A displaced Torontonian Jim is a storyteller in the best Grand Manan tradition. Certainly anyone who lives in a mansard-roofed, Gothic-style mansion such as the Marathon Inn would have to be a believer just by default.

It has been fifteen years or more since Jim introduced Mystery Weekends to the Maritimes. In addition to well-plotted murders, Jim takes great pleasure in sitting by the huge fireplace in the "Annex" and telling his favourite tales about Grand Manan, its people and its ghosts.

Logic would demand that the Gothic inn, perched as it is at the top of the hill in North Head and looking like a picture on a Hallowe'en poster, would be home to the unknown of the spirit world but logic seldom prevails in the matter of ghosts. It is, rather, the Annex which is alleged to be home to mystical wandering gentlemen with courtly manners and workmen with noisy hammers.

Equally as strange is the fact that, though Jim tells the stories, it is the guests in the Annex who see the apparitions and hear the strange noises. Jim just sets the scene, as it were, repeating the tales his guests have shared with him. ››

Guests and 19th Century strangers meet on the Annex stairs

There are times when the ghosts are pretty active, I get complaints about footsteps in the hall at all hours of the night. A couple, who were here with their kids, complained that the coat hangers in the closets were swaying for no reason, lights that were turned off, turned on by themselves. They blamed the kids at first until they realized it was happening when they weren't anywhere near.

Rooms 35 and 36 appear to be the focus of activity. One guest sensed someone behind her going up the stairs to the third floor one night. When she turned around a man dressed 'funny', not fancy in any way just 'funny' or 'strange', glided by and disappeared in the hallway above.

The apparitions could be caused by the three workmen who died under mysterious circumstances while they were moving the Annex from the area called Marble Ridge at the top of Moses field. Appropriately called the *Marble Ridge Inn*, it was won in a poker game in 1898 by Captain James Pettes, who built the Marathon in 1871. He moved it and another small house he owned at Pettes Cove here to his own property and they became the Annex.

No one knows for sure what exactly happened to the three workmen, whether one of the buildings slipped its moorings and fell on them ... whether it was an accident or deliberate. Only one of the three remained behind to haunt the premises from time to time. No one knows why.

Those who have seen the ghost describe him as looking more like a French peasant than a turn-of-the-century English workman. There are those, too, who believe he may have come with the Annex when it was moved and not, after all, be the ghost of one of the workmen.

Regardless of his origins he has given a thrill or a fright to more than one guest at the Marathon Inn ... sometimes he has also had a little help from some friends.

Jim Leslie suggested that I should ask New Brunswick photographer Freeman Patterson, who often holds workshops at the Inn, about some of the ghostly experiences, enjoyed or otherwise, by aspiring photographers.

Here are Freeman's contributions to the Marathon Inn ghost stories. ১১

One woman from Toronto attending one of my workshops was very susceptible to any ghost story she was told. As a result the ghost seemed to have a special interest in her.

At three o'clock one morning she woke up and jumped out of bed in alarm ... her bathtub taps were running. She turned them off but, as soon as she was back in her bed, the taps in the sink started running.

The water finally stopped running but she was not back to sleep for long before she was rudely awakened again, this time by dogs howling and a racket coming from the ceiling above her head. The noise finally ended on the sound of a big jet coming in to a screaming landing.

I have never known of even a small jet landing on Grand Manan. Other people swore they didn't hear a thing but she was suspicious, and rightly so I think. How much of that nonsense was ghosts and how much was her fellow photographers I leave to you to decide.

I later learned that one of our photographers was an expert sound technician. ১১

The Pirate at Long Pond

While sceptics may question the Marathon Inn ghosts it takes a strong person to argue with Vernon Bagley of Seal Cove, Grand Manan when he starts telling of his experiences with the unknown.

Oral historian Janet Toole of the New Brunswick Archives interviewed Vernon in July of 1992. A natural story teller with a lively sense of humour Vernon enjoys a healthy disrespect for just about everything, including dead bodies and their ghosts.

Here is Vernon's story of the Pirate at Long Pond, paraphrased and edited for clarity and space. ⁊⁊

Well, up around the shore, I used to tend the bird sanctuary. I was a warden ... and a fire chief too, at the time. So I had all I could handle.

This day I remember I was wearing a shirt, with the shirt sleeves rolled up, and I had my binoculars with me and I was walking over by my cabin when I saw there was a bird out on the outlet of that pond. It was flippin' around and I thought that something was wrong with it.

I was looking through my binoculars when all of a sudden, right out by the side of him, I see this man coming towards me. From the ocean side, it was.

I kept hauling the binoculars way out and looking at him and here it was a man with his overcoat on!

Thinks I, 'For the love of Mike, what in the world is this comin' toward me?'

The closer he got the funnier I felt. And I looked at him and he was dressed just like a pirate. He had a long coat on, he had a sword hangin' on him and it was hangin' below his coat, not in a sheath.

It was right there, swinging back and forth.

He had a red bandana around his head and he kept

strutting. He came up from the ocean, but he wasn't wet. And he strutted right along but he never looked at me once yet he was coming right towards me.

He strutted right along that shore road and I could see that sword switchin' back and forth and he came right up alongside me and the closer he got the queerer I felt. He had on leather boots and them all a-shining and that long coat, on a warm morning like that. I just couldn't understand it. And he walked right up and never eyed me once.

He never winked. He never blinked or anything. He wasn't looking at me, he was looking right by me.

Well, I like to greet a fella a little bit when I meet him and him so close ... and I thought I spoke to him half-decent ... but his cheeks swelled out and he let the mightiest roar out of him ... just like a lion.

And then he walked down to the woods. Now if a fella's gonna hide from you he always looks around, to see if you're watching him. He didn't. He just stepped into the woods and away he went, out of sight.

Well, it was only a narrow strip of woods and the pond was on the other side of him between the woods and my cabin.

Thinks I, 'Why would a man roar at you if you spoke to him half-decent?' 'And I thought I did.'

So I says to myself, 'I'll go over there and wait 'til he comes across that space and then I'll have another talk with him. I'll tell him what I think of him.'

Anyway, I went over to that space and he never showed up. So I looked everywhere in that bunch of trees but he just seemed to vanish.

About that time a car drove over and it was a police car. So, I come out of the trees.

'Bagley,' he says, 'what are you hunting for?'

So I told him the whole story.

'Well,' he says,' you know a man can't hide from us

over here.'

I said, 'I can't find this critter that just walked up along side me a few minutes ago and roared at me!'

And we never found him either. He just vanished! And I've never seen him since ... and I don't know as I want to.

The next time I heard about him there were two kids, they went over and they built this big fire over there, along on the beach. They had it going quite a little while so there was a lot of red hot coals there and they were toasting weiners.

There was a little mist on the beach and by-and-by this kid looked up and here was this fella standing right there ... just outside the fire a little ways. This kid got scared and he made his feet go jiggling and his weiner went down into those red hot coals, see? And the two kids were both still looking at that fella and with his bare hands he hauled them red-hot coals apart and picked that weiner out of there.

Well with that they were scared so bad they just jumped up and run as hard as they could go.

I heard about this story and I thinks, 'I'm gonna call those kids.' They lived in North Head if I remember right.

This little fella was so excited on the phone he started right off going right to town on the story!

I said 'I want you to explain how he was dressed and what he looked like.'

He piped up and he said, 'He had a round nose!'

And he did, too. He had a nose rounded like an eagle's beak, that fella that walked up the beach did.

'That's the same fella, all right.' I said.

Where did he come from? That's what I'd like to know.

My uncle said he thought he must have come to see if his buried treasure was still there. I said. 'I'll hunt for it then.' So I did. But I never found it. ɴ

Mrs. Huestis' wooden leg

When Frank Allard bought his Chatham Century Home there were many things about it that intrigued him. First of all, it was an 1850s coach house converted into a dwelling. This lent itself to an interesting room layout. False halls were 'inserted' in the centre to partition the rooms, jigs and jogs were added for kitchens and porches. The second floor was divided, quite simply, into two big rooms with a loft above. ▷▷

As far as I can tell we were only the third family to move into this place. We bought it from a couple named Ross, prior to them it was owned by the Huestis family.

The previous owners had not completely cleared everything out from the upper areas when we took it over. Mr. Ross said it was mostly old junk that had been there from the year one and offered to come over and get rid of it. I said not to worry, I'd just heave it all.

It was just junk, but in with the junk was this old wooden leg. I didn't want to throw it out because it sort of intrigued me, but I didn't want my wife to be upset either. I suspected she wouldn't take kindly to having an old wooden leg hanging around the house.

I really did want to keep it. I thought it might be a fun thing to have around for Hallowe'en, say, or just for a joke. So I put it away in a dark corner. A short time later I was in Montreal and my wife was puttering around upstairs and she found the wooden leg ... She freaked!

I said 'Okay! I'll get rid of it!'.

I hated to see it go. It was quite elegant looking, full-length with a foot and all but made out of wood and it looked homemade compared to the fancy hard plastic ones they have these days. Anyway I took the leg and I put it in the neighbour's garbage.

That night I woke up to a loud thumping noise coming from the second floor. I knew there was no one up there but I went up and looked all around, checked the windows to see if it was windy and something was blowing against the house. There was nothing. There was absolutely nothing that could have made that noise.

I went back downstairs and, no sooner was I settled in bed than it started again. *Thump ... pause ... thump.* It kept up all night long, punctuated in between the bangs and thumps by the occasional crash, as if something had fallen.

It occurred to me then that maybe it had something to do with the wooden leg. It *sounded* for all the world like someone with a wooden leg walking around upstairs.

I convinced myself it was my imagination and eventually got back to sleep but the thought stayed in my mind.

The next day I did a thorough check of the house, everywhere. Inside and out. There was nothing anywhere near that house that could have been making the noise I heard the night before.

The next night and the next night the same thing happened.

I decided the wise thing to do would be to go next door and see if the neighbours had sent their trash to the dump yet. If they hadn't, I would get the leg back and maybe that would be the end of it.

Unfortunately I was too late. The garbage was gone.

Feeling sort of sheepish and stupid I casually started asking around about the people who had owned the place in the past. It was then that I learned that Mrs. Huestis, one of the former owners, had a wooden leg!

I began to have visions of being wakened and tortured every night by a crazy, imaginary wooden leg thumping around in the attic because it had been separated from its owner. Or was it Mrs. Huestis thumping around because I threw her wooden leg out? I stopped trying to figure it out!

One night I even got up and went to the stairs and called up to her. I was beginning to get desperate and my wife was not happy at all. Mrs. Hucstis didn't answer but for a couple of days after that we did have some peace and quiet.

Some friends and I even tried to get a séance together, to see if anyone could contact her but we couldn't find a psychic. I'd really like to know if it is Mrs. Huestis stomping around up there.

I wondered what I would say to her if we made contact. Something like "I'm sorry I put your wooden leg in the garbage?"

I'm serious. I know it sounds funny but I'm really not making a joke about it.

I have been living in that house now for eleven years and, while it doesn't happen every night, the sound of that wooden leg walking around has now become a normal part of my life. I've got so I don't even hear her... or it ... anymore.

Sometimes there will be weeks or months between visits, at other times the racket will go on for days and weeks at a time.

Frank became so accustomed to Mrs. Huestis' wooden leg prowling around the attic that he tended to forget about it being there. During the 1993-94 school year he took sabbatical leave and rented the house but neglected to tell his tenant about Mrs. Huestis and her

wooden leg. I was doing my research during the time Frank was away and had heard the story of the wooden leg from his friends. As a result, I talked to his tenant, Norman Liaro, before I talked to Frank.
Here is Norman's story. ঌঌ

I had heard Frank joking around with Allan Irving about a Mrs. Huestis and her wooden leg but I don't think I ever paid a lot of attention to what it was all about. It just seemed to be some sort of joke they had going between them.

After I moved into the house I heard a lot of strange noises and a loud '*thump*' that sounded at times as if someone was pounding on the floor with a sledge hammer but there were other unusual noises too. I thought it must have something to do with the wind roaring around the old place.

Once I woke up in the middle of the night when I heard a huge thump that seemed to come out of nowhere. The whole house shook. I couldn't imagine what it was. Thinking back, I suppose it could be the sound of someone falling but at the time I didn't identify it, I was just annoyed at being awakened in the small hours of the morning.

I play a lot of music and I got used to all the noises, but my girlfriend was uneasy about it and that made me a bit edgy sometimes, I admit.

I tried to convince myself that it was just the wind but I guess I knew better, although I still hadn't connected the noises to the wooden leg but once someone told me the whole story of Mrs. Huestis and her wooden leg I felt better about everything. I have sympathetic vibrations with ghosts, after all I grew up with them when I lived in Montreal.

Our house had been in my mother's family for generations and she insisted it was full of ghosts. I never saw or heard them, the only people who ever did hear them were my mother and other women.

But my mother swore that every night she could hear her father come upstairs to bed and I believe her.

As for Mrs. Huestis and her wooden leg, I was just glad to finally know what all the racket was! ঌঌ

A Restless Spirit at Millbank

Like a number of people who have contributed to this book, Jenny Bruce of Douglastown was born with a cowl or veil over her face.

"I was born at home," she said. "My mother had a hard time giving birth but she was finally delivered by the midwife who told her that mine was a strange birth. I remember my mother telling me the midwife peeled a diaphanous material from my face and held it up to her, saying, 'This is very strange!'

"She then draped the material over the oven door to dry but apparently the heat ruined it."

*Until Jenny read Joanne Cadogan's interview with me in the **Miramichi Leader**, in which the mystery surrounding such births was discussed, Jenny had never given any thought to her mother's story or to the cowl which covered her when she was born.*

She now feels that the things that happened in her lifetime, that she always attributed to a woman's sixth sense, just may have been more than that. What significance, if any, the cowl at birth may have had she doesn't know. Nor can she begin to understand why these experiences happen to her and to others, or what they mean. ➳

I knew I had what I thought of as a *sixth sense* that all mothers develop. Throughout my life I attributed numerous fortuitous experiences to this. It was actually responsible for averting what could have been a chilling and tragic happening.

We were living in Toronto at the time and I was teaching school. The twins were young enough to still be in diapers on the particular night that remains so vivid in my mind. I had bathed, fed, then tucked them in bed before leaving for a Home and School meeting,

I can remember so clearly walking through the living room to the door, assuring my husband that the children were all settled in and that I doubted he would hear anything from them while I was out. I was at the car door when something made me turn around and go back in the house directly to the children's room.

One of the twins was convulsing and frothing at the mouth. We called the doctor and rushed him to the hospital where he was immersed in a cold bath and his temperature brought down to normal.

Apparently he has an internal temperature that can't tolerate the least fluctuation. Until then we knew nothing about this. His temperature was normal before I left but if my sixth sense had not kicked in he would have been dead by morning.

I had difficulty giving birth and the doctor did not want me to have any more children. This was back in the 1960s when the birth control pill was very new on the market and the doctor was confident that they were safe and were just what I needed.

I believed that the pills were making me hemorrhage. One day the hemorrhaging was so bad I was rushed to the hospital emergency department and put under an anaesthetic while they attempted to stop the blood flow.

The whole time they were working over me I could see and hear everything that went on. I remember hearing the doctor say, *I can't stop this … I'm going to lose her … then* suddenly there was a loud ringing noise and then the ringing stopped and I went down this tunnel with lights at the end. But I never reached the lights. I woke up.

I told the doctor what had been said and done while I was under anaesthetic and he couldn't believe it. But he couldn't deny it either because everything I told him they talked about was exactly what had been said and done.

'You were supposed to be under anaesthetic,' he told me.

Jenny's strangest experience was more recent and more stunning because,after keeping it to herself for years, she discovered that her husband had had the same experience, in the same place, but at a different time.
Here is Jenny's story as she wrote it to me: ÞÞ

A cousin of mine, to whom I was not particularly close, was accidentally killed at a loading dock in Millbank about ten years ago. The circumstances were particularly tragic. He slipped off the back of a pulp truck and into the ice-covered river but the hole in the water was large enough to permit him to plead for help until the strong current carried him under the ice, to the utter dismay of those trying to rescue him.

Although I was saddened by the event, it was not something that particularly preyed on my mind.

I was attending a meeting in nearby Chatham on a very warm summer night. I rolled the windows down to cool off the car, turned on the radio and leisurely proceeded towards home, passing through Millbank on the way.

When I reached the area where the accident had happened I suddenly felt a cold breeze. I didn't find this unusual as we're used to the east wind coming up fast and dropping the temperature drastically in a very few minutes.

I rolled up the windows but, instead of feeling warmer I felt colder. I turned on the heat but it didn't help. The inside of my car was icy.

I began feeling very uneasy. My heart was beating fast, my hands were sweaty and, most disturbing of all, I could feel a presence in my car.

It overwhelmed me.

My mind kept saying, 'this is impossible. You're just tired, keep going.'

I looked in my rear view mirror but I could not see anything. I had a hard time keeping my hands solid on the steering wheel and I kept telling myself to look around to the back seat. But I hesitated to do that.

Suddenly, the name of my cousin, *Yvon* popped into my head.

I slowed down and turned toward the back seat, I knew then that he had been the presence. The car warmed up immediately. I turned the heat off, rolled down the windows and went home.

I never told anyone about this incident until one night, after my husband and I had watched a program on *Unsolved Mysteries*, we started discussing ghosts and other unexplained events. To my utter amazement my husband disclosed the following incident:

That same summer he was travelling to Heath Steele Mines, north of Newcastle. Usually he travelled with other workers in a van but that particular night he decided to take his own vehicle. When the shift ended he left for home.

Again, it was very warm ... then he suddenly felt very cold and did all the same things I did, rolling up the car window ...turning on the heater ...

He related how totally consuming the cold was and how a presence made itself known. At first he thought he was hallucinating because he was so tired.He was hyper-ventilating, sweating and very cold. Suddenly, he thought of Yvon and the cold ... the presence ... immediately disappeared.

My husband is not prone to believing things he can't understand so this was particularly disturbing to him.

We were amazed that, for so many years, neither of us had mentioned the incident for fear of being either laughed at or accused of making it up. Now we feel relief in realizing it really happened, that Yvon was restless, due to the very tragic circumstances of his death. ◌◌

The bad luck house in Loggieville

Theresa Kelly would like to put memories of the house in Loggieville, where she and her family lived for over four years, out of her mind.

"It's a bad luck house," she says. "Everyone that I know who has lived there has had bad luck."

Theresa herself had the worst kind of luck you can have, her three-year-old son was killed when they lived there.

"We didn't have any children when we first moved there and I guess I should have moved right out at the first of it because it was scary from the beginning, living there. But you got used to it after awhile."

Originally, the house had been a one-family dwelling but it had been turned into a two-family home over the years and, as a consequence, a set of stairs between the two levels was boarded up to ensure privacy.

"The noise came from those stairs. The people upstairs were pestered by it more than we were, we could only hear it when we were in the living room. Upstairs they could hear it all over the house, in the bedrooms worst of all."

The noise was not a banging or thumping sound, and it wasn't the sound of someone walking around. It was the sound of a baby crying.

"We had been living there for about a year when our son was born. He was just a little feller when the woman upstairs came down one day looking as if she had been through a wringer.

"You do look a sight," I told her.

" 'You should too,' she said. 'That baby of yours kept us awake all night!'

"I told her she must have been dreaming, that the baby had slept like a lamb all night."

From then on the sound of crying kept up on a regular basis. Theresa could be sitting in the living room with a quiet baby on her lap and she would hear the crying infant's wails coming to her through the walls.

She got up one night to warm her son's bottle for him. While in the kitchen Theresa was startled by a "terrible racket" she said was coming from the kitchen cupboards.

"I had just cleaned those cupboards that day and I couldn't imagine what could be in there, unless it was another ghost! So I shouted, 'You stop that right now, Frank ...' and the noise stopped right away.

"I tell you, I was some scared at that. I said it part as a joke because the house had been built by Frank Loggie, one of the founders of Loggieville. When the racket stopped right away I grabbed that baby's bottle and high-tailed 'er out of there. Fast!"

Theresa never heard the noise again and she had two more children while living there, before disaster struck.

Her oldest son was three-years-old and he was standing beside a telephone pole, watching some street repairs going on in front of the house, when he was struck by an oil truck and killed instantly.

"I never slept another night in that house," Theresa said. ﷼

Mama smiled when she heard the footsteps, 'Dave's back,' she said

Betty Irving and her sister Louise Girvan's child-hood home was at Flatlands, near Campbellton, about a mile past Morrissey Rock. Although the house was torn down five years ago both the ghosts they grew up with and those they live with now, are an accepted part of their lives.

Betty says she firmly believes everyone's spirit settles some place. "You leave your imprint. That has to be it but I don't pretend to understand. There's another life going on all around us, we just don't get to see it."

Both women shared their many stories with me, regretfully space doesn't permit telling them all at this writing.

As we waited in her Loggieville kitchen for Louise to arrive from South Esk Betty began the narratives. ᎒᎒

People say to me, 'Betty, doesn't it bother you? Having all those ghosts haunting you?'

I ask them what's to be bothered about? ... There's no harm to the ghosts no matter who they are. I'm so used to them they don't bother me a bit.

I'm a ghost in my own house. My 20 year-old daughter Sharon is so convinced of it she no longer sleeps in her bedroom. She prefers the discomfort of a couch when she comes home from Fredericton.

She keeps waking up in the middle of the night and seeing the spectres of her father and me standing together in the bedroom, like we're talking about something but she can't hear us.

I tell her it can't be my ghost, I'm not dead yet even if her father is.

But she insists. 'It's you Mom. You're standing there talking to Dad then you walk away, right through the wall, and disappear.'

It's not a vision she has only seen once, it appears regularly, that's why she won't sleep in that room anymore. It's the only place she sees the images.

But Auntie Margaret is one of my favourite ghosts. She was always a good Catholic but she made Baptists out of the family after she died.

She was my father's Auntie Margaret, my Grandfather Ferguson's sister. She died in the family home at Flatlands before the priest got there to give her the last rites of the Catholic church. When he finally arrived he told my grandfather he wanted $3,000 to administer the rites and told him she couldn't be buried in the Catholic cemetery unless she had them.

Well, my grandfather's name wasn't Michael Ferguson for nothing. He was about as Scotch as you could get and he said the priest wasn't getting any $3,000 out of him. So he took Auntie Margaret over to the Baptist church and had her buried in the Protestant cemetery.

From then on Auntie Margaret haunted the house, no doubt irked at her brother for not coughing up the money for the priest.

My grandfather also haunted the house at Flatlands after he died and he's been both seen and heard by several members of the family.

Some people used to be terrified to stay there. It

was a big house, there were 17 rooms in all, nine bed-rooms plus the downstairs rooms.

The first time I heard my grandfather was one night when my children were younger and I was home alone with them. Everyone else had gone to a church supper and I was sitting alone in the living room, in the dark, with just the fireplace going. It made it cosy, the way I liked it.

The house was quiet and I was sort of daydream-ing until I was startled out of it by the sound of someone coming out of my mother's and father's bedroom. I knew it wasn't Auntie Margaret because whoever it was, was wearing heavy boots as he walked along the upstairs hall and down the back stairs.

I called out, 'Is that you Dad?' but no one answered. My father and mother had gone with everyone else to the church supper.

I didn't think to say anything about it when they came back because it was my turn to go to the supper and leave them to mind house. The next day I did ask my father if he had come home for anything and when he said no, he hadn't, I told him about what I heard. He said it sounded like his father, who had died in that bed-room. He said my grandfather was never known for pus-syfooting it around anywhere.

I had heard *about* my grandfather but it was the first time I had actually *heard* him!

I never did see him but two of my children did.

One night when Allan and Dorayne were playing in that selfsame living-room they looked up to see a big man with grey hair and a beard walking into the room. They said hello and asked was he looking for someone but he didn't say anything, just turned and walked away.

They told us he came down the stairs, through the living room and the dining room and out to the kitchen. They never thought anything about it because there was always someone coming or going around the house, the doors were never locked.

It was my brother, their Uncle Verne, who said the description fitted our grandfather to a 'T' ... I never saw him, even when he was alive, because he died the year I was born, but Verne did. He said he was a big man with a grey beard. He was 92 years old when he died.

We didn't see or hear too much of him but Auntie Margaret walked around steady. All the time. She was restless, probably because she wasn't buried in the right cemetery.

Aunt Louise was my father's sister, she was just a little girl but she had good reason to remember Auntie Margaret when she was alive. She said she was real hateful, a witchy old thing. Her bedroom was the one up over the kitchen and she never gave it up after she died.

One time Aunt Louise was playing in the kitchen and she did something near the stove that resulted in her clothes catching fire. Auntie Margaret just sat there and watched them burning on her and didn't do a thing to help. My grandmother came out to the kitchen, fortunately, and saved the child.

She really did look like an old witch, Auntie said. She was tall and lean, had a hooked nose and black hair.

Anyone who was living in that house when they died came back to it. There was Auntie Margaret, Grandfather and my father. I didn't ever see Daddy but I heard him. My sister Louise says he was heavy on the right foot and Grandfather was left-footed, that was how you could tell them apart.

Louise , the oldest of the seven Ferguson children, maintains that the family ghosts have followed her around through the years.

"I think it's either Daddy or Grampa, or maybe both, somehow I can't see it being Auntie Margaret, there's too much fun to it," she said as we talked over tea at Betty's kitchen table. ♪♪

My first cousin, Elizabeth, is the only one I know who ever saw Auntie Margaret. She was about six years old and had gone upstairs to play, after being given strict orders not to meddle. Well there she was, meddling in someone's dresser drawers, when she heard a noise behind her. She turned around quick, guilty like, and there was Auntie Margaret standing there with her hands on her hips.

Elizabeth flew down the stairs to the kitchen. She was sick to her stomach and white as a sheet. We knew there was something wrong but she never told anyone until she was sixteen years old. She and her mother were looking at a picture of Auntie Margaret and that's when she told her what happened that day.

The day we buried Daddy we were all sitting around the kitchen table, it could sit 24 easy, and Mama was reading a letter from Daddy's brother in Quebec. Daddy was seventy-six when he died and the other brothers and sisters that were there started arguing about how old everyone was. Finally, Aunt Louise who was now the family matriarch, settled it all because she was the one with the family Bible.

Everyone shut up then and for a few minutes there was quiet, just long enough to hear footsteps going from the bedroom down the hall to the bathroom.

Mama nodded her head and smiled.

"Dave's come back," she said. ♪♪

The Ghost at Platt's Point

Harry McCleave, who divides his time between Hampton and the family home in Rexton, has been devoting considerable effort lately to genealogical research. In the course of his research he was fascinated to discover the following ghost story among his mother's papers.

Marjorie Jardine (Thompson) McCleave lived much of her life in Moncton and Halifax raising her family and following a career as a librarian. She returned to her home in Rexton in later years and, Harry says, encouraged people like John Orr to write down the stories they told her.

It is one of John Orr's stories that we repeat here, much of it taken from the handwritten original found among Marjorie's records.

Harry said he thought it was written sometime in the mid-to-late 1930s, when John Orr was in his fifties or sixties.

"I know the ship he wrote about was destroyed in 1887 and he would have been around ten years old at that time. As far as I know he died in Loggieville in the 1960s or 1970s. He was a real storyteller."

I have of necessity paraphrased John Orr's story, using the occasional direct quote in order to retain the flavour of the storyteller's words. ▓

Dream Town becomes Ghost Town

In the early part of the Nineteenth Century the government of New Brunswick put a trunk road through from Chatham to Shediac. Prior to that the road was a mere bridle path. (*It is now a part of Number Eleven Highway.*)

The road struck the bank of the Richibucto River a short distance above Platt's Point on the north side of the river and it came out halfway between Beatties' Creek and Tomson's Creek on the south side. The government of the day established a ferry there consisting of two scows, two small boats and two double-log canoes. These craft were propelled by hand with oars and paddles and there was a small slip built of logs on either shore to provide a landing area for the scows.

The people of Kent County believed that the ferry was the first step to the community becoming a village or town and envisioned the building of a bridge as the next step, all of which would lead to prosperity for the citizens.

Mr. George Platt, from whom the point takes its name, decided to be prepared for progress and built a wharf and a store on the point. He reasoned that, since nearly all trade in those days moved by water, his success was highly probable.

At about this time William Girvan, a young Scotchman who came from Galloway with his parents, arrived on the scene.

"Mr. Girvan was a man of powerful build and possessed lots of ability, which he afterwards showed. Like a number of others with the same idea, he thought that a Ferry would bring a boom to the shores of the Richibucto."

So he built a good-sized store on the south side,

near the slip. Then he built a large twelve room house a short distance up the road, leaving some very large Spruce trees in front of the house which gave the place a very attractive appearance. He also built a large barn and a warehouse in back of the house.

Everyone expected the dream of a town and a bridge would soon come true. Which it did. Not, unfortunately, at Platt's Point but two miles up the river, a short distance above Hughes Point.

The ferry was soon discarded and Mr. Girvan saw that his trade was gone. Unperturbed by the turn of events he rented his house and went to Saint John, where he prospered greatly and was soon appointed president of the Bank of New Brunswick, a position he held until his death.

Mrs. Sennett, from Prince Edward Island, rented the house and took in shipyard workers from her native province as boarders until that industry, too, began to wane.

It was after this that the ghost made its first appearance of record.

Mrs. Sennett sublet some of the rooms in the northwest end of the house but her new tenants did not stay long. They complained of loud rapping and mournful sounds in the night and complained loudly. At first their landlady did not put much stock in their complaints and the tenants moved out.

Mrs. Sennet rented it to some other people, only to suffer the same complaints and to have these tenants move out as well. Before long the word was out that the Girvan House was haunted.

"There were two men boarding with Mrs. Sennett. One was from the old country and the other was from P.E.I. These men kept a watch out to try to catch the Ghost.

"They took notice that there was a white boat with a new sail down in the bay about dark on the nights that the ghost paid his visits. So one day Marton Ladiner, for that was the name of the man from P.E.I., said to his mate, whose name was Bill O. Mahar, 'you being an Irishman ought to be able to lay a ghost.'

"Bill said 'sure if I had about a cup full of tar and a small handfull of Ockem I think I could do the job.'

"So Marton, being a caulker by trade, filled a small dish of tar and put a small amount of Ockem in his pocket and took it with him."

A short time before dark the white sail appeared down the bay and the two watchers went down to the shore and sat in a fir grove. Along about midnight they saw the boat coming near a sand point. A rather tall man stepped ashore and put a small anchor in the sand. Then he walked up the shore.

"Marton walked along in the bushes to see where the stranger was going. He got to the upper end of the grove so he stopped and kept an eye on the house. After a while he began to hear queer noises but he could not see his man. He was at the lower side of the house so he took a look to see if he could see the boat from where he was.

"He saw a small black puff of smoke rise out of the boat followed by a bright light and all at once the boat was wrapped in flames.

"Marton looked toward the house and he saw the tall man from the boat coming down the shore as if the prince of the world was after him. The man took one look at the boat and kept on down the shore as fast as his legs would carry him.

"Bill said, 'Sure I think the fire laid the ghost,' and he passed a flask of whiskey to Marton who asked him where he got it.

"Bill replied, 'I got it under the after thwart of the boat. I saw it shining when the fire started'."

Some time after the above adventure Mrs. Sennett again rented the rooms, this time to some dressmakers. Within a short time the ghost began its knocking again.

One of Mrs. Sennett's boarders, a Mr. Maloney was coming back from Kingston and, as he walked down the Ferry Road, he saw something all in white dodging around in the woods. Moving quietly he went around the house and into Mrs. Sennet's barn where he got a short ladder. He placed this against a big spruce tree near the northwest corner and crawled up the tree and lay down along the lower and largest limb and waited.

Before long he heard a noise below him.

It was the ghost and he passed below him and made for the first window.

"It was all white and it had something waving over its head. First it made calls as if it was a cat. Then there were a few moves and the long white thing began to scrape across the window.

"Well, Mr. Maloney thought the limb would be all right to slide down to the ground so he let himself go ... his aim was better than he expected for his big brogans landed right on the ghost's shoulders.

"The sheet went one way and the poke went another and the ghost went down with the wind knocked out of her!"

The story goes that when the woman got her wind back she began to plead with Maloney for mercy. Maloney relented and gave the sheet back to her and advised her to "go home and sin no more".

Apparently Maloney never did divulge the name of the "ghost" which probably accounts for the rest of the story.

From the time Maloney toppled her until Mrs. Sennett sold out and went back to Prince Edward Island the ghost never made another appearance or a sound, which led some to surmise that Mrs. Sennett herself was the ghost of the Girvan house.

Such was not the case.

Shortly after Mrs. Sennett and her tenants left, a family named Henderson arrived by schooner with all their worldly goods and took up residence.

It was not long until the ghost once more set to work ... but always when Mr. Henderson was away from home.

The family decided discretion was the better part of valour and packed their goods and chattels and moved on to, presumably, a less haunted environment.

The next resident was "a big powerful man by the name of James Scott and none of the ghosts seemed to want to have anything to do with him for the Scotts were not bothered while they lived there."

Mr. Scott was the last official tenant of the house but the ghost stories connected with the Girvan house on The Ferry Road don't stop there.

John Orr writes that the 'harpies' (bill collectors) came and began to look for their rights. First they carried away the store, then the warehouse, then the barn and finally they began to carry away the house. They took away all the windows and all the doors except for a door on the pantry under the fruit stairs.

"By this time the older generation had either passed away or left the area so the ghost stories were about forgotten until one day a family by the name of Mackentire arrived and moved into the old Bell house, not far away from the haunted Girvan House.

"Mr. Mack was a fisherman and one day he hired a youth from Galloway to come and haul some wood out of the woods.

"The boy's name was Oswal Young, a sturdy chap

brought up on oatmeal and the shorter catechism. He had never heard anything about ghosts but, when he arrived, Mackentire's two boys, Jack and Jim, joined him and went to the woods for wood. At noon time they put the horse into the barn to feed and went to get their dinner. After dinner they went to the barn and Master Young began asking questions about the old house across the way. So they invited him to go over and see it.

"There was quite a lot of snow on the ground so they had to wade through it to get to the house. In the meantime an elderly man named Thomas Bell, who lived up on the back road, came down to Mackentire's to hire Oswal Young to haul some wood for him.

"When he enquired where they were Mrs. Mackentire told him they had gone out to the barn. Mr. Bell saw their tracks when he went to the barn and followed them to the Girvan House and looked in. There was no one in sight but he could hear the boys talking upstairs. Thinking to play a prank on them he went in the pantry and began to thump on the stairs and howl like a cat.

"The young Mackentires yelled 'a ghost!' and ran for the back stairs and out the door. Oswal was at a loss as to which way to go so he went down the front stairs as fast as his legs would carry him.

"When he reached the floor he saw that the pantry door was open so he put his shoulder against it and closed it with a bang. Looking around he spotted a plank on the floor so he put it against the wall and jammed it down against the pantry door. After that he ran for the Mackentire's barn, got his horse and drove to the woods for more wood, picking up the Mackentire boys at the old school house.

"They wanted to know if he saw anybody. Oswal said 'no' but that he had put the ghost in cold storage for the winter."

According to Orr's story, shortly after Oswal's horse went out the gate Mrs. Mackentire went to the well for water and she heard someone calling from the old house. Her husband was fixing his net and when she told him her story he went over to the old house to see what was going on.

"Before long Mr. Mackentire located the source of the noise, pulled away the plank and opened the pantry door under the stairs. Out walked Mr. Bell, well covered with cobwebs and feeling rather cold. Mr. Mack laughed and asked him what happened."

"Mr. Bell shook himself and said, 'There's no fool like an old fool! That boy Os. was too smart for me ... but don't forget to tell him to come and haul the wood for me!'"

The old house was taken down a short time later and all the old ghosts went with it and there were no more ghosts for a long time.

A few years ago there appeared to be a ghost on the north side of the river. He seemed to have his head-quarters at or near the old trotting park but he did not stay very long. Whether he was connected with the ghosts of the Ferry Road or not John Orr said he had no means of knowing.

A Ghost of an Idea

*The foregoing ends John Orr's story from his hand-
written notes but Harry McCleave takes up the tale from
there.* ♪♪

The latter day ghost mentioned in Orr's notes re-
fers to the 1930s when there was a lot of bootlegging
going on in the area. It is said that a plan was concocted
by bootleggers to have ghosts appear which would draw
crowds and police away from the area while booze was
being unloaded near Platt's Point.

A correspondent for the Moncton papers, got a lot
of mileage and some money out of the reports he prepared for the *Moncton Times and Transcript.* The stories,
in their turn, attracted would-be viewers from Moncton
to the area.

As a result, many people travelled down our road
and soon became damned nuisances to my grandmother,
who had a weak heart and didn't want to be bothered
with them.

The nuisance (and the ghost) disappeared when
my uncle, Burpee Jardine, returning from a day of hunting found the entrance to the lane blocked with sightse-
ers. When they told him the ghost had appeared down
the lane he removed his shotgun from the car and, with
a great show, loaded it. He then drove slowly down the
lane ....

After that there were no more incidents of tres-
pass! ♪♪

Moncton's ghosts that might have been ... or still might be

Searching for ghosts in the Moncton area can be compared to looking for pie-in-the-sky, a blue moon or a needle in a haystack.

Moncton Tourism's Audrey Williston told me the closest she could come to ghosts was some thought of developing 'kindred spirits' at the Capitol Theatre ...

Audrey suggested I call Charles Allain at the Moncton Museum, a possible source of ghost material. Charles confessed that ghosts in Moncton were in short supply. He did come up with a story about a cousin's cottage where the door would open and close and steps could be heard walking into the cottage at night but the story had never been developed nor the occurrence researched.

Charles and Audrey reinforced what I already suspected, that if there were any ghosts in Moncton the only person sure to know about them was Ned Belliveau.

Ned, whose historical research under the name of J.E. Belliveau has kept the people of Moncton and Shediac in touch with their past for five decades, soon set me off in the right direction.

At first, when we talked on the telephone he suggested that "maybe the realities in Moncton were too strong to foster the imagery of ghosts.

"Moncton has a wholly different tradition from those of Saint John, Fredericton or the Miramichi. People here were transients in the beginning, workers in the shipyards then later for the railways. The people were commercial-minded, there was very little romanticism."

Later, he wrote:

"I'm not certain whether you wanted real ghosts

or situations that engendered ghostly ideas. So, on second thought, I thought I'd draw your attention to two or three things that might fit your theme whether apparitions appeared or not ... they certainly did in people's minds."

He spoke of the ritual slaying of Mercy Hall and the crazed people set off by Jacob Peck in his religious seances.

"The whole Shediac Bridge settlement saw ghosts then."

Like much of what follows, the story has been well-documented by Ned in his book *Running Far In.*

In the letter he also spoke of Capt. John Friar of Shediac, a sea captain who sailed the Moncton-built Lalla Rookh to the Far East where he was devoured by cannibals when his ship put into Hoopiron Bay at Moresby Island, New Guinea on July 2, 1885 ... his ghostly ship came back to Shediac minus the crew.

"There is a memorial stone to him in the Greenwood Cemetery at Shediac/Pointe du Chene. As I tell my grandchildren, 'The only grave of a man eaten by cannibals'."

Speaking of memorial stones, Ned shared with me the story of the gravestones that disappeared from the old Presbyterian cemetery abandoned more than a century ago.

"When I was a boy there were four standing gravestones there. They are gone now, and I know where the last two went!

"The late Allan Tait confided in me that he and Dr. Bill Webster, once head of Canada's national science centre and one of the physicists who worked secretly on the British/American atom bomb, snuck into the field after dark one night and spirited off the Chapman stone, marking Webster's grandmother's grave, and a stone marking that of another relative. He said this was so that the family could be reunited, ghostily if you will, in the Greenwood Protestant cemetery where early and late Taits and Websters lie."

He went on to suggest that one might look in the old Presbyterian cemetery to see if the ghost of British Prime Minister Bonar Law's minister-father is floating over the forgotten graves there. Apparently the senior Bonar Law preached at the old kirk.

The racing spectre

Ned's grandmother, Catherine Anketell, told him this story about the little girl who was killed by a passing train, where the railroad tracks cross Hall's Creek at Sunny Brae. One of the two little girls in the following story was Ned's grandmother who, coincidentally, later married the same Peter Leger of the story. 🙰

Just before the time of this story, a little girl had been killed by a train on the trestle at the place where the railroad tracks cross the creek at Sunny Brae.

A man, named Peter Leger, walking from Sunny Brae to the Salter shipyards slipped over the same trestle and hung onto the jutting ties, narrowly escaping the same fate as a train thundered toward him.

On this particular summer evening in the year 1877 the two young women, neighbours of Mr. LeBlanc, were walking along the marsh road to Lewisville near the trestle. They were always apprehensive when in the area and were startled and frightened when they saw a ghostly figure swooping down the embankment toward them.

They were sure they were seeing a ghost!

Stopping dead in their tracks and holding their breath as the apparition drew swiftly nearer they saw that it was wearing white shorts, a white shirt and running shoes.

And with relief they recognized him. It was Ned Henderson, a legend in Moncton, doing his roadwork.

Known as "the fleetest foot in the whole region" he was to race 100 yards against Fred Harmon of St. Stephen, known as the "fastest human in the Maritimes" for $500 a side.

Unfortunately for Henderson, Harmon won.

The haunting story
of Shediac's Smith family

In his book, The Splendid Life of Albert Smith, Ned weaves a fascinating story around the women in the life of this former provincial premier, the most fascinating of whom was his great-granddaughter, Caroline deLancey Cowl. At the time of her tragic death she was known in Fredericton as deLancey Torrie. If anyone deserved to have a ghost to be remembered by it would have to be this woman. The story begins ninety-five years before deLancey's death. ≫

"It was a night fit for skulduggery, dark and windy. On that night of October 12, 1878, the body of Mrs. Thomas Edward Smith of Shediac Cape, New Brunswick, was snatched from its grave. She was the mother of the most famous man of his time in the province, Sir Albert James Smith, knighted by the Queen that very year. Local legend said the lady's body had been buried with jewelled rings on her fingers. The mystery has never been solved.

"... ... To this day, people of the district do not mention the victim's name, only that the body of 'a prominent local person was stolen,' from the churchyard of St. Martin's-in-the-Woods.

"The mystery is compounded by the fact that on the same night a year earlier, on October 12, 1877, Tim

McCarthy, a money-carrying cattle buyer, was murdered in the bar of Shediac's Waverley Hotel and the killing was never solved.

"On the same night, a year later, October 12, 1879, the entire business district of Shediac was destroyed by fire. For years afterward on each October 12 the streets were patrolled throughout the night by vigilantes."

Marjorie Young Smith, great-granddaughter of Mrs. Thomas Smith and the mother of deLancey Torrie, eventually inherited two family fortunes and married another. By the time her father died the family may, justifiably, have become somewhat superstitious because Marjorie's mother dropped a canister containing his ashes into Shediac Bay, rather than risk a cemetery burial.

Four years later Marjorie obliged in a similar manner for her mother but more sportingly, according to the family caretaker who confided to Ned that she "kept the ashes on her bedroom dresser all that winter and when spring came paddled out alone in a canoe and just dropped them over."

Then, on October 29, 1973, ninety-five years after the body of the first Mrs. Smith of Shediac Cape was snatched from its grave, the mysterious death of her great-great granddaughter, deLancey Torrie, a 55 year-old, twice married, twice-divorced recluse, was reported in the *Fredericton Gleaner.* There was no obituary, just a paid notice, which did not say that she had died of starvation or that, apparently unknown even to herself for it is not included in her will, she had left behind an estate worth more than a million dollars ... and jewellery (her mother's famous two strings of Hearn pearls) which sold at auction for $120,000.00."

Her mother, Marjorie, who divorced deLancey's father and later married the extremely wealthy Ralph Pickard Bell of Halifax, had left more than seven million dollars to Mount Allison University in Sackville!

Whether deLancey did the honours for her mother in the traditional manner is doubtful. Professor Fred Cogswell, said he knows she got letters from her mother but he doesn't believe she ever read them or answered them.

"The brilliant, high-strung, over-trained thorough-bred poor little rich girl was the only one of Sir Albert Smith's sparse family who seemed to have inherited any of the reformer's social consciousness, and she was incapable of doing anything with it," in Ned's opinion.

For twenty-one years deLancey lived as a recluse in Lonsdale Court in Fredericton. A compulsive night person, in time she became a severe psychotic with signs of schizophrenia.

For years Prof. Cogswell, who had published some of her poetry in *The Fiddlehead*, and his wife brought her groceries and befriended her, as much as she would allow but her demands finally became too much for them.

"She would often make us wait for hours before permitting us to bring the groceries into the house then, once we were inside, she would insist that everything had to be evenly distributed in the various rooms, according to some set pattern in her mind."

A Mr. Neales delivered oil to the house and was the only one who managed to persevere and continue to supply her with her meagre groceries. The last time he entered the house he found her dead.

Shocked, he went outside, collapsed in the yard and died at once. Two ambulances arrived and the street was agog with the excitement and speculation.

" .... The funeral was like a Gothic travesty. With Professor Cogswell there were three other pallbearers, one her lawyer, one her doctor, one her banker. A member of her stepfather's family came and thirteen others."

After reading Ned Belliveau's fascinating story, which I have drawn from both liberally and gratefully, I find it hard to believe that deLancey is resting peacefully somewhere. Her's did not seem to be a spirit at peace with the past or the future, let alone her own time.

Does she haunt the family home in Shediac? Or does she continue to live at Lonsdale Court, still faithfully served by that kind soul, Mr. Neales? ༒

About the Author

Dorothy Dearborn began writing as a child and published her first poetry and short stories in the 1950s. A television career, as writer and host of a talk show, was interrupted by six years of active politics.

She worked as a reporter and later served as city editor of *The Evening Times-Globe* and editor of *The Kings County Record* and *The Saint John Citizen*.

Among her many interests are the promotion of literacy in New Brunswick and acting as chair of the Southern New Brunswick Area Legal Aid Appeal board.

Mrs. Dearborn continues to work as a journalist. Her articles are regularly published in newspapers and magazines nationally and internationally as well as within the region.

When not searching out stories for her articles and books she can be found in front of her Macintosh computer at the family's 19th Century farm house in Hampton, in the company of her aging Newfoundland Dog, Tillie, an ancient pony named Soupy and a motley assortment of other critters.

She is married to Fred Dearborn, they have four grown children and several grandchildren.

About the Illustrator

Carol Taylor of Rothesay, is a New Brunswick figurative artist who works primarily in clay and oil. She has recently been commissioned to do a three dimensional interpretive clock for the historic Saint John City Market.